BLUES

DAVID R. GODINE: PUBLISHER   BOSTON

BLUES

Robert Neff & Anthony Connor

First published in 1975 by David R. Godine, Publisher
306 Dartmouth Street, Boston, Massachusetts 02116

Copyright © 1975 by David R. Godine
Photographs © 1975 by Robert Neff
ISBN   0-87923-152-1, hardcover
       0-87923-153-x, softcover
LCC   75-11468

Printed in the United States of America

BLUES was designed by David Ford. The type, Century School-
book, was set by Dix Typesetting Company. The paper is Mohawk
Poseidon Text. The book was printed and bound by Halliday Litho-
graph Corporation.

Grateful acknowledgement is made to:

Marvelle Music Co., New York, N.Y. & Hollywood, Calif. for
permission to quote "Cleanhead's Blues" by Eddie "Cleanhead"
Vinson.

Crossroads Music Co. for permission to quote "Livin' with the Blues"
by Brownie McGhee.

Arvee Music, a division of The Everest Record Group, Los Angeles,
Calif. for permission to quote from "Long Gone Like a Turkey
through the Corn" by Lightnin' Hopkins.

Testament Music, Pasadena, Calif. for permission to quote from
"Tom Green's Farm" by Johnny Shines.

Pamco Music, Inc. & Sounds of Lucille, Inc., New York, N.Y. for
permission to quote "Why I Sing the Blues" by B. B. King.

Modern Music Publishing Co. & Sounds of Lucille, Inc., New York,
N.Y. for permission to quote "Sweet Sixteen" by B. B. King.

Modern Music Publishing Co., New York, N.Y. for permission to
quote from "Boogie Chillen" by John Lee Hooker.

For Kathleen Neff

ACKNOWLEDGMENTS

We are grateful most of all to the musicians who were so generous with their time and cooperation and made this book possible.

In addition we would like to thank Jim and Amy O'Neal; Bruce Iglauer; Steve Tomashefsky; and Bob and Susan Koester who offered both their help and hospitality while we were in Chicago.

Special thanks to David Foster and all the people at *Shaboo* for their generosity and faith in the project.

Finally, we are grateful to Kathleen Neff for her constant support and for the long hours she spent helping with the transcribing of tapes and the editing of the final manuscript.

INTRODUCTION

On a hot summer afternoon in Harvey, Illinois, we talked with slide guitarist, J. B. Hutto, on his shaded front porch. Where we sat was cool and comfortable, and maybe his optimism was at least partially a reflection of his enjoyment of the day. Nevertheless, when we asked him about the future of the blues, he said, "The blues will never die cause it's the original thing. It's coming back up from where they tried to stomp it down; it's coming back up again, and it's gonna get better. Blues will be blues until the world ends!"

J. B.'s prediction for the future may not be shared by everyone, but his statement reflects the kind of hope and toughness that keeps the blues alive. But the blues tradition, which is mainly oral, grows more perishable each year. Little Walter, Otis Spann, Elmore James, Magic Sam, Earl Hooker, Sonny Boy Williamson, Arthur Crudup, Junior Parker and scores more have died in recent years. Others are in shaky health. We've worked on BLUES with a strong sense of lost time and vanishing opportunities. However, for audiences interested in America's fundamental music form, it is still possible to see and hear musicians like Muddy Waters, John Lee Hooker, Lightnin' Hopkins, B. B. King, and others who are, without question, major figures in this country's cultural heritage.

For two years, we followed the blues whenever and wherever our time and money would permit. We talked with musicians in their homes, in motel and hotel rooms, backstage at theaters, in bars and parked cars. The words and photographs which come from these talks taught us about the musicians' lives, and the book evolved because we wanted to share this experience. The blues is basically a vocal music, we have tried to make BLUES an extension of that tradition.

Thus, BLUES is not a musicological treatise. Neither is it a history of blues or a study of individual artists. Rather it is a mingling of the voices of scores of blues musicians, who talk about their music, their pasts and their futures, hopes and fears, failures and ideas. All the musicians we talked with are not necessarily "legends," but each has something to say, and their collective voice tells not only about the blues but about a particular time in the Black American experience. The stories span, roughly, four generations, from the Depression through the early seventies, and follow a general geographical path from the cotton fields of the South to the industrial North with its related troubles. Across this space and time stretches a fabric of shared experience, attitudes, and traditions. It is at once a tough but hopeful music, a music of rare spirit and passion. Here, we have tried to let musicians speak as the music itself speaks—directly to the listener—and we hope that the reader will find, as we do, that the remarkable blues men and women in the book literally make the pages sing.

Robert Neff
Anthony Connor
May, 1975

Brownie McGhee   I don't write anything from imagination. Blues is not a dream. Blues is truth. I can't write about something I haven't seen or experienced. Whiskey, women, money, maybe politics—these are my leading topics.

The highway has been my home. I haven't been in prison for murder, but I do know what a jailhouse is. And I do know about gambling, and I know all about riding in the back of the bus. I tell people about this.

John Lee Hooker   I have had some weird experiences, and that's where I get my songs—from my hardships and experiences with people. And *women*. Women have caused me heartaches and problems. I've been so easygoing to my women, and then I find out things wasn't going my way. And it puts a lot of sorrow into me. Then I can think and make songs built upon these misfortunes. It ain't only women. You might lose your money or your beautiful car. Or can't pay the house rent. And you sing these sad songs to ease your mind.

Every song I sing is something that happened to my life or somebody else's life in this world. If it ain't hitting me, it's hitting *some*body out there. Every person or every race have had these heartaches and tribulations in life.

That's why everyone digs the blues . . . it has more feeling than other music. When I sing these songs I feel them down deep and reach *you* down deep. I have a lot of soul for this, because I have crossed some rough bridges. Sometimes it didn't look like I'd *get* across, but I got across somehow. And I never for*get*. The memories are still there, and that's what my songs are built up around.

Now I'm on this side of the bridges, and I know there are more ahead. But I wouldn't go back for nothing. I wouldn't try to cross them back again. But they're in my songs . . .

Brownie McGhee—*Shaboo Inn,* Mansfield, Conn., 1974

Brownie McGhee Sometimes the life I was living in my younger days would've drove me to crime, but I couldn't escape. "How can you rob this bank?" I said. "You'll get caught. No way out." So I took the other way: I suffered. Being honest with myself, I knew I couldn't go out there and dig ditches; I was handicapped. I had polio. So I suffered. And I didn't give up.

That's the message I'm trying to get across in my music today: "Don't give up! Your day will come, but you got to be strong and survive until that day."

From my childhood living with the blues to where I am
*   now,*
I'm not gonna worry,
I'll get by somehow.
My mama had them and my daddy had them, too.
I was born with the blues.

You think I'm happy, but you really don't know my
*   mind.*
You see a smile on my face,
but my heart is bleedin all the time.
My mama had them and my daddy had them too.
That's why I was born with the blues.

Rocks have been my pillow,
the cold ground has been my bed.
Blue skies have been my blanket,
and the moonlight's been my spread.
But I'm not ashamed. Ain't that news!
I been living with the blues.

That's the story of my life.

B. B. King
WHY I SING THE BLUES

Everybody wants to know why I sing the blues,
Yes I say everybody wanna know why I sing the blues,
Well I've been around a long time, I really have paid my
*   dues.*

When I first got the blues, they brought me over on a
*   ship,*
Men was standin' over me, and a lot more with a whip.
Now everybody wanna know why I sing the blues,
Well I've been around a long time, mmm, I've really
*   paid my dues.*

I've laid in the ghetto flats, cold and numb,
I heard the rats tell the bedbugs to give the roaches
*   some.*
Everybody wanna know why I'm singin' the blues,
Yes I've been around a long time, people, I've paid my
*   dues.*

I stood in line down at the County Hall,
I heard a man say, "We're gonna build some new apart-
*   ments for y'all."*
Well everybody wanna know, yes, they wanna know
*   why I'm singin' the blues,*
Yes I've been around a long, long time, yes, I've really,
really paid my dues.

My kid's gonna grow up, gonna grow up to be a fool,
'Cause they ain't got no more room, no more room for
him in school.

And everybody wanna know, everybody wanna know
*   why I'm singin' the blues,*
I say I've been around a long time, yes, I've really
*   paid some dues.*

*Yeah you know the prophet he told me, yes, you're
   born to lose,*
*Everybody around me, people, it seems like everybody
   got the blues.*
*But I had them a long time, I've really, really paid my
   dues,*
*You know I ain't ashamed of it, people, I jes' love to
   sing my blues.*

I walk through the city, people, on my bare feet,
*I had a fill of catfish and chitlins up and down Beale
   Street.*
*You know I'm singin' the blues, yes, I really, I jes'
   have to sing my blues,*
*I've been around a long time, people, I've really, really
   paid my dues.*

*Now Father Time is catchin' up with me, gone is my
   youth,*
*I look in the mirror every day and let it tell me the
   truth.*
I'm singin' the blues, mmm, jes' have to sing the blues,
*I've been around a long time, yes, yes, I've really paid
   my dues.*

*Yeah they told me everything would be better up the
   country, mmm, everything was fine,*
*I caught me a bus uptown, baby, and all the people
   got the same trouble as mine.*

I got the blues, uh, huh . . .
*I say I've been around a long time, mmm, I've really
   paid some dues.*

Blind man on the corner, beggin' for a dime,
*The roller come and caught him and threw him in jail
   for a crime.*
I got the blues, mmm, I'm singin' my blues,
*I've been around a long time, mmm, I've really paid
   some dues.*

*Oh I thought I'd go down to the Welfare and get
   myself some grits and stuff,*
*But a lady stands up and she says, "You haven't been
   around long enough."*
That's why I got the blues, mmm, the blues,
*I say I've been around a long time, I've really, really
   paid my dues.*

Johnny Shines Lots of things we call blues today really isn't the blues. Most of the things you hear are love songs: "She got big brown eyes, she got pretty golden hair, she got big legs, and I love her—she's so tender, her heart is made of gold," you understand? And we call this stuff "blues." But we're not talking about our state of being—things that are happening to us.

The blues are not wrote; the blues are *lived*. Here's a boy born a millionaire—the onliest way he can have the blues is if he lose it all and, boom! he's thrown flat out on his face. Then he's gonna have the blues.

When you hear people singing hymns in church— these long, drawnout songs—that's the blues. Yeah. Church music and the blues is all one and the same. They come out of the same soul, same heart, same body. The division come back in slavery times when slaves were singing these mournful, lonesome songs. The slaves didn't know anything about "blues" or "church songs" at that time.

We were brought over here as slaves. We didn't bring no instruments, no sheet music—nothing but what we remembered in our minds. What happened to the older ones that were brought over here? They were soon *dead*, because what man from Africa had learned how to get out and work twelve and fourteen and fifteen hours a day carrying logs, cleaning up ground, and digging ditches, working with ice and stuff? It took a younger man who had to be hardened as he come along. And these were the men who were singing the blues, even though they didn't call it that.

They learned English. They sang songs about the food they was eating, the way they was living, how they was getting grippe, how they was louse-y . . . these people didn't even have no clothes to change into! Lice ate them up, you understand? And they was full of disease. And these people didn't have no syphilis station where a Black man could go and get a shot if he caught syphilis or TB. If he had pneumonia, they made horsehoof tea for him . . . they didn't call in no doctors for this man.

Then these people singing these songs begun to be noticed. The White people started asking, "What's wrong with these people? Why is they singing?"

They didn't know these people really was praying, that every time they opened their mouth was a prayer coming out—that every word was a story. So how could it be called "blues" or how could it be called "church songs?" They asked, "What's wrong with these people? They sound like they have tears in their voices."

So the masters held a meeting about it—said, "We got to do something about this. Tell these people, 'Don't sing those songs. Don't sing about your state of being. Sing about John the Baptist over the sea. Sing about the holy city—Jerusalem. You'll be so happy when you get home over the river Jordan.'"

The White people taught them these kind of songs. They taught them the Bible. They stopped them from singing about being beat and full of lice, and sickness, and death, and sold.

Just think of a little child standing at his mother's knee, crying, "Mama, take me up." And she can't even look down at him. She's got to look the people in the eye who's gonna sell her and buy her. "Mama, please, I want some titty, Mama." She can't even reach down and pick him up and nurse him.

Now, those people had the *blues*!

When they told them they shouldn't sing these songs, they told them they was reels. "Don't sing those reels or you'll die and go to hell and burn forever and ever." And then they went on later to relate those reels to syphilis, sex, murder, getting drunk—you understand what I mean? And naturally the people believed them. Who else was there to believe in?

They was taught they was the wrong color, until they got to the place where they hated their own selves. They maybe hated the other man, but it come out they hated them*selves*. See?

We was taught if you was Black, you was wrong. This got to the place where we would put all different kinds of stuff on our faces, trying to lighten our skin. We hated black.

Even now, the average Black man wants to be called "Black," but you ease up to him and say, "You *black* son of a bitch," see if he don't knock you down. But still he wants to be called a Black. It's a lie; he learned to *hate* being black.

Now here's a *real* blues song'll show you what I'm talking about. It's about Mr. Tom Green's farm.

If Mr. Tom Green didn't feed so good, I'd
*   leave right away.*
I'd go to Chicago to the bright lights, and
*   that's where I would stay.*

Man, if you miss your sweet woman, you can bet
*   your hat,*
go to Mr. Tom Green's farm. That's where you'll
*   find her at.*

The last verse talks about this color brainwash thing. It ends up:

If you stay out of the ground, Mr. Tom Green'll
*   keep you out of jail.*
So you better be careful what you say about
*   my eyes,*
else the ground hogs'll be bringing you your mail.

In other words, I'll kill you. If you tell me my *eyes* is black, I'll kill you.

And this is what really happened on Mr. Tom Green's farm. Those guys over there would come over here on this plantation and take your wife and bring her back to their farm. And you better not go over after her, because there wasn't any law except don't steal nothing from the *White* man and don't be caught with no *White* woman!

If you killed another Black man, they'd just say, "We got to split his land up between you and so-and-so and so-and-so, cause he's dead now."

"Yassuh, I'll take it. I'll work it."

Sing about *that*. That's the real blues.

Johnny Shines—New York City, 1974

Roosevelt Sykes Do you believe in God almighty and Jesus Christ and the Holy Ghost? Do you read the Bible?

I've been religious since I was thirteen. Baptized then, in 1919; and when he stamped me, I stayed stamped. I got with the highest thing and stayed there.

I couldn't *make* it if I had to go by myself. He gives me everything. He gave me talent: I didn't pay a nickel for it. He gave me knowledge enough to know what he want me to do—I'm a blues player. When it comes down to my work, it's music—jazz, blues, boogie. That's what I work to deliver. And with this talent, I travel all around the world, stay in the finest hotels, ride the finest airplanes from coast to coast. He give it to me, so I praise him.

I've had my fun. He made this earth for man to have some fun in. Enjoy. The one thing He don't want you to do is mistreat a man or woman. He love people. He want you to love one another as he love you. I love all people. I love everything God made. I pray to feel that way. I want to be the best loving man in the world.

God will always be the heavenly father and the ruler, as long as you see that sun rise and that moon at night. As long as the tree have leaves, He will be king. Cause he is life.

Willie Dixon I was raised up on blues and spirituals; but after you wake up to a lot of facts about life, you know, the spiritual thing starts to look kind of phony in places. So this is one of the reasons I guess I took off to the blues. I liked the blues and I stick to the blues, because the blues gives you a chance to express your feelings. And it's wrote on facts . . . not phony.

The older people always considered the blues sinful music. They used to say you were singing and playing the *reels* if you sung other than spiritual songs. It could be *any*thing— love songs! If it wasn't spiritual songs, they called it reels, and this was considered sinful music—dancing music.

You know, the Black people in America had all their things they got from the white slave owners down

there; and the owners would tell them anything they wanted to, to *use* them with. They had to control the slaves any way they possibly could. And they wanted them to believe praying was going to help them in the next world. They was brainwashing the Black people with spiritual ideas—teaching them the Bible and telling them about how they could fly to heaven and all this kind of stuff.

When I was a little boy, my mother said if you crossed the River of Jordan, you was in heaven. I mean, these things sound so impossible, and most people don't believe them. But I remember when I was little—when we was going to Sunday school—they all had songs about standing on the banks of Jordan and cast a wishful eye . . . and everyone got happy on this thing. They figured if they cross the River of Jordan, that was their homeland and heaven. This is what these old people had in mind, you know, because this is what they were trained and taught to believe.

Years afterward, after I came to Chicago, I went to Israel with a music tour, and I brought back a Bible and some letters with postmarks from there. And my mother couldn't understand how in the devil did I go to Israel, you know, and Jerusalem. *Espec*ially Jerusalem! Because the Bible had a lot of Jerusalem stuff in there. When I got back from the tour, I told mama, "There really is a Jerusalem and a River of Jordan, because I *been* there. And they have more gambling in Jerusalem than in the United States; and most of the crooks they can't find in the States, they're over there!" And she just couldn't understand it . . .

Willie Dixon—Chicago, 1973

Brownie McGhee When I was little, my daddy moved us from Knoxville to Kingsport, Tennessee, where he got better work. He was a common laborer, and he helped to build that town. It was a cow pasture when we moved there.

There was a lot of blues and hillbilly around, and my daddy played with a mixed group. They played country music and old hoedowns and things, calling sets, and women in long dresses jumping around. When you saw above a woman's ankle then—man, that was a miracle! Mostly they danced on hard ground, out in the barnyard or someplace; houses wasn't available. We had a ball, though. We'd be beating on cans and playing one-string banjoes and blowing kazoos and playing fiddles and guitars.

My daddy was a blues singer. He sang "Betty and Dupree" and "Stagolee" and he told me about these men cause he knew them; and I thought it was a fairy tale till I found out that others knew them, too. His singing was mostly about his everyday life—his hard work and his pay and how he disliked the boss; how the pressure was put on him; the condition of his hands. And I realized in later years what he was talking about when he'd come home tired, and after a meal he'd lean back in his chair and start picking his guitar. And I liked it.

I heard him a lot at house parties, too. My daddy was a heavy drinker—on the weekends. That was his big thing. He was a hard-working man, but when he was off, his pleasure was to have a few drinks with friends and play his guitar.

I started off playing *his* guitar— when he wasn't around. I didn't know the keys, but I'd bang around with it. I loved that guitar—getting sounds out of it. When I got it out of tune, he figured out what I was doing. At first he was mad, cause his guitar was very important to him; but later he taught me some—how to pick it, not just strum it.

I really picked up my style from him cause his blues sounded mostly just like talking. He didn't rhyme his lyrics. He just sat there and sang about what happened that day. He made me very interested in what was going on in life.

Phil Guy My dad, he loved the blues, you know. He had records by *all* the old blues cats, man. He had Smokey Hogg, he had all of Lightnin' Slim's records, and Lightnin' Hopkins, and John Lee Hooker—oh, man!

He wrote a lot of tunes—*good* tunes—and Buddy, I think, cut one or two of them. They sounded kind of old and funny back when Buddy first started playing, so I guess he didn't really get into them until recently. Now he looks at them and thinks about how all this stuff begins to blend in; the times changed so much, and so many people have got into the blues, you know? Really got into the blues more and more.

Whenever Buddy'd come to Baton Rouge with his group, my dad and I'd always go to see him. And before my dad died, he did get a chance to come up to Chicago and stay around for a while and see Buddy play.

His dream was for Buddy and I to get together and play. He always wanted that. And that's just what we're doing now, but he didn't live long enough to see it.

Buddy Guy   I've got a kid working with me, a free-lance photographer, going back where I was born, getting hold of old pictures and stuff. My mother's mother passed away two years ago this month; my father's mother's brother is still living down there. And I want to get to some of these people. Maybe they can tell me something about myself I can't get any other way.

I just wish my father was living, man. He was the type of guy that encouraged us in whatever we do. Like I used to love to play baseball and box, and he used to say, "If you want to do it, *do* it. But if you ain't gonna do it, no sense bullshitting with it. Leave it alone."

And he used to encourage rivalry. He used to signify a lot between Philip and I. He'd go up to Philip and say, "Well, it don't look like you gonna play anything tonight. I guess I'll have to call Buddy." And then he'd do the same damn thing to me! He was always a signifier like that, to try to make us do better, keep us grudging at each other.

He remembered all the old tunes by people like Ma Rainey. He tried to get me to do "Stagolee" long before Lloyd Price sold a million copies of it. But every time I'd get to the part about "he shot Billy," I'd say, "Hey, what am I gonna do with that? And he said, "I'm telling you to take this song, cause that's all they're recording is the old stuff over again, and do it in a new style." But I couldn't make no sense out of it then. My father did give me one of the best tunes I ever had as far as sales-wise in Chicago: that line about—Muddy used it, too—"Goin' back down South where the weather suits my clothes—"

I haven't been baptized, but I believe in a lot of the things my parents taught me. My daddy was a Bible man. You couldn't ask him *noth*ing, he'd tell you what verse to go find. He straightened my wife out with that shit. She reads it herself a bit, you know. One time

they got in an argument; she was telling him he was wrong. And he sat there till she was finished, and he said, "Now go get your Bible and go to page so-and-so, and I'm gonna tell you how it reads." And he read it without the Bible, Man!

Just before he died, he told my sister there was something he wanted to tell me, something he wanted to talk to me about. But my sister figured I was trying to take care of my family in Chicago, so why make two trips down South? So they waited till he died, then called me to the funeral. But I wouldn't have cared about the two trips, man; my father said he wanted to talk to me, that's what I cared about.

My mother and father always told me it's best to come up the hard way. And I know some people, I won't call any names, is well off, and their kids is fucking up. They don't know *what* to do. But if you come through some of the things *we* come through, when you get hold of a dollar, you value it. If you drink it up, you better enjoy that drink.

So I'm never gonna give my kids everything they want. I'm thinking about getting the older one a paper route now, but I don't want nobody messing with him, and you know how Chicago is: you got old-ass people come around and bullshit with a little kid, which is something *I* better not ever see. But I'm on the road most of the time, so who knows what can happen?

I't not only Chicago; *all* big cities are full of that shit now. People's just not living like my parents lived. Even my wife'll tell me sometimes that I'm old-fashioned. But I still think that was the best way.

I really want to go back to Louisiana and buy a little ranch—five or ten miles out of the city, not way out the country with the damn crickets and frogs—'cause there's a much slower pace down there. I'd just do it for my kids.

Dave Myers   My brother Louis always has been very serious about playing the guitar, but I started out sort of later. I was always a good *dancer*. I'd go to parties and dance like hell, and all the girls liked to dance with me. But I didn't really think about music till my family got to Chicago from Mississippi in 1940 and I started to go round to different places and hear music. And the sound kept a-beating into me. And it just got down *into* me where it forced me to try it.

I had left my parents' home at sixteen, and I was working in a restaurant and looking out for myself, when one day this old winehead sold me this guitar—talked me into it. He was playing on the corner for dimes and nickels, and he looked over and saw me setting on the damn steps of my apartment house. So he said, "Hey, how would *you* like to hear a good tune? Just give me a dime, and I'll play you something you never heard." Well, naturally I wanted to hear him, so I give him a dime. And he started rapping on the guitar. Sure enough, he was making some mighty good sounds.

Pretty soon he said, "You give me another dime and I'm gonna show you how to do just what *I* did." So he taken my hand and placed it on the strings, and it felt pretty good to me. I was enthused about it.

So we fooled around there, and after that he talked me into buying the damned guitar—for four dollars. He said, "Now, I'll come back tomorrow and give you back the money and get my guitar." I never saw that guy again.

So he stuck me with the guitar. And I got working and plunking around on it. And so help me—here I am.

Hammie Nixon   When I was eleven years old, [Sleepy] John [Estes] come up my side of town [Brownsville, Tennessee] playing for a picnic. I was blowing my little ten-cent harmonica, and he heard me and I guess he liked it. So he asked me to help him, and I earned me a dollar-fifty. I thought I was a big man.

Well, when we got through playing, somebody'd hired him for a dance, so he said, "Stick with me. I'll ask your mother." He promised her to bring me back the next day.

So he carried me to the dance, and I made another dollar and a half. So we kept on across the river into Arkansas.

Well, we had such a big time in Arkansas, that we kept on into Missouri. We sounded pretty good, and he told me I could make it. I was getting better all the time—started blowing jug, too.

When he finally brought me back, he told my mother, "He's *good* now." And I had enough money in my pocket to buy her a big old twenty-four-pound sack of flour. So she wasn't too mad.

So me and him went off again and stayed six months.

That was almost fifty years ago, and we been going off together ever since.

Honeyboy Edwards   Joe Williams came to Greenwood, Mississippi, in 1932, when I was around seventeen. I was small, just a little skinny thing—looked about fourteen. He played at a country dance one Saturday night, oh, about half a mile from my house, across the fields.

So I stood back in the corner and listened to Joe Williams play. He had a good punch to his blues at that time: he could play that guitar!

Well, I told him I could play.

So he said, "You want to try a little?" So I took his guitar and played.

Then he asked me where I lived, and I told him across the field. So he come home with me that night after the dance. Got acquainted with my father and everything. Said, "I want Honey to go off with me. I'll learn him how to play guitar."

We weren't working in the fields at that time 'cause it was winter, so my father said okay.

I had an old guitar with the neck busted off, so my brother and I glued it back together and put new strings on it.

So I just left like that with Joe Williams, started playing around. We traveled to Vicksburg, Natchez, New Orleans, down along the Gulf Coast—riding buses and hitchhiking, with guitars on our shoulders—just going.

We made a pocket of money—three or four dollars here, three or four yonder. People was glad to see us come, cause there wasn't too many blues players out in that country at that time.

I'd be shooting marbles with the other kids while he'd be drinking and running round with the women. He always had plenty of women, but sometimes they caused him problems. He's have two or three in the same place sometimes; and one'd get hot, and another'd get hot, and he'd be trying to keep them separated. He just was an old playboy.

He used to be a *tough* fellow too. Gee, he wanted to fight and clown all the time. He was just crabbish and got mad easy. I liked him though and he liked me. He knowed my whole family.

He was just like a father to me, really. When he had money, he'd buy me things. And he taught me all about playing blues.

After about a year like this, I left Joe in Columbus, Mississippi, over near the Alabama line. I came home to Greenwood, and I really thought I knew how to play then.

Esther Phillips One of the happiest times I ever had was the first time I played the Apollo. I had just recorded "Double Crossing Blues," and everybody thought that was Dinah Washington's song, so on all her jobs they were asking her to sing it.

Well, when I hit the Apollo, she had a box seat. I had never seen her, and they told me she was there. I said, "Oh, my God, is she?" Johnny [Otis] said he was going to introduce her, and I said, "No, no, please let me do it!" So I introduced her and she came down on the stage, and I asked her if she would do a song for me. She had a red purse which she asked me to hold for her, and she sang.

When she got off, she cussed Johnny out. At thirteen, I was very developed for my age, but they had me in bobby sox, ribbons, and braids. She told Johnny to take those braids out of my hair, take those bobby sox off me—the shoes were alright; she approved of the shoes. And she took me to dressing room number six, which was the star's dressing room at the Apollo, and she curled my hair and got me some hose. She told Johnny, "You got her up there looking like a goddamn fool!" That was one of the happiest moments of my life. She did me an extreme favor.

And then the second happiest thing that happened to me, as far as Dinah is concerned—she gave me my first Mr. Blackwell gown. She always used to give me clothes and things, cause I was growing up and she could see I really didn't know how to dress. And my mother didn't know how to dress me.

She even *insulted* my mother! Among other things, she told my mother that everybody was stealing our money. She said, "I can understand that you don't want to hear this, but I'm gonna say it and I don't care whether you like it or not: they're stealing your money—stealing *your daughter's* money." My mother was furious. But when she found out it was true, of course she had to have the greatest amount of respect for Dinah.

Doctor John My earlier recording sessions were more straight blues dates—those little ten-dollar-a-tune dates—or ten dollars for the whole session. Then in fifty-six I joined the union, and after that I started doing union sessions and legit records with the real pros—people like Roland Cook, or Huey Smith or Charles Brown, or Amos Milburne.

Chess, Arrow, Fury records—all them came to New Orleans for a lot of recording work, and they used to call me in all the time. I recorded with all kinds of people—Big Boy Miles, Eddie Bole, Bobby Charles, James Booker and his nephew, Jimmy McCracklin, Bobby Hebb, Little Willie Johns, Eddie Lang, Al Johnson, Mercy Baby, Paul Gayten, Roy Brown, Barbara George, Carol Fran, Bernadine Washington, just about anybody who was recording in New Orleans. Junior Parker was one that I had an opportunity to work with, who was my sweet-blues-singing idol. Dave Dixon—he

Doctor John—Boston, 1974

just passed away—he was another great one, one of the great blues ballad singers. He did some all-time classic records, man. He was a great originator, but he never got the recognition until he became one of Huey Smith and the Clowns. Cause groups were the big thing at that time.

I cut with everybody, man. I was doing sessions every single day, there was so much business coming to New Orleans. I can't even keep track of it.

You know, there's this cat in Paris—a record historian. When we was in Paris, I talked to him; and he knew a thousand times more about the sessions I played on, the whole scene, than I *ever* knew. And what *he* had fitted exactly in with what *I* had. And this cat had every record I every played on or produced or arranged and records that to my knowledge were never even released in the states. The dude would be saying, "Yeah, you played piano on this, guitar on that and so and so played the saxophone." Man, I was amazed. Here's some cat in Paris, France, who knew more about shit we were doing in New Orleans in the fifties than I did when we was doing the shit.

Actually, the musicians I was playing with were more important than the artists we were backing. That was my schooling, man.

I cut with Sonny Boy Williamson one time and I didn't even know which Sonny boy it was. I didn't care. The name didn't mean anything to me then, other than he was just an old man cutting.

I did get excited though when I had an opportunity to cut with Charles Brown. Oh man, I got so excited and scared about that! On the first date I showed up drunk and got fired. To get to play with Charles Brown, man—that was just too heavy for my little teeny-bopper brain to handle.

Willie Dixon   Little Brother Montogomery, I would say, was my first contact with music altogether.

I had heard guys singing the blues up and down the streets, and we'd go out in the country and hear people sometimes; but Little Brother, he used to always be on a wagon bed or a flat-bed truck. There'd be a piano up there and a set of drums, and maybe horn and guitar players. A guy had a megaphone and hollered where they'd be playing that night, and Little Brother would play. And I'd be running behind the truck or wagon, barefooted. I was only seven or eight years old, and I'd be out there running after them all day. My mother'd give me a whipping when I got home.

Boy, that guy can play a lot of styles on piano! He can play peoples' styles that nobody's heard of before because they was never recorded, but he met them all when he was a little kid. That's why they call him "Little Brother," cause he was a baby playing with all those old guys. I heard him talk about musicians like Papa Lord God, Chicken Shoulders—you never heard such names in your life! They've all been dead for years and years.

Little Brother Montgomery   I admired a million musicians since I was small and on up until now. A lot of them are dead, but I still love them. Now when I was little, I admired Jelly Roll Morton, Papa Lord God, Blind Homer, No Legs Kenny. All these kind of people were great piano players. We had a lot of them from New Orleans. So many, I just can't name them all. Kansas City too.
You used to have thousands of musicians were great

around Chicago too, such as Hersal Thomas that was Sippie Wallace's brother. He was a great piano player. Teddy Wilson, Earl "Fatha" Hines, Clarence Jones, and a man who made most of his living playing pool—we called him "Toothpick"—Ted Waterford, Cripple Clarence Lofton, Sweet Williams: all these people were great piano players. Fats Waller, used to live on Michigan Avenue, was one of the greatest piano players ever. He played hokum and stride. Pinetop Smith could play a great boogie, till he got killed. Clarence Jones had the pit band at the Grand Theater. Erskine Tate had the band at the Vendome. There were bands all over the city. We had some great guitar players in Chicago then, too—Charles McCoy, Joe McCoy's brother. Robert Junior Lockwood—that's my buddy. Some of these people are still around if they ain't dead.

I still know people all over Chicago that I knew when I was six and seven years old, playing for Sunday parties at my parents' house in Kentwood, Louisiana. Willie Dixon lives near me: I knowed him ever since he was about eight years old—big, fat boy running around Vicksburg, Mississippi, following us and trying to hear us play. I knowed his whole family.

I knew Jelly Roll Morton, too, in the South and in Chicago. He used to play in my father's juke in Kentwood on weekends. He'd play Friday and Saturday and go back to New Orleans Sunday or Monday. He gave me my first piano lessons. In Chicago he used to hang around on Forty-seventh Street with the piano players, drinking moonshine. He always had a thousand-dollar bill in his pockets somewhere; and then he had diamonds on his fingers and all in his shirt and in his teeth and a .38 special in his bosom. He was nice; he just like to brag.

We had a lot of great singers back there. Before Lonnie Johnson all the great blues singers were women.

Little Brother Montgomery—Chicago, 1973

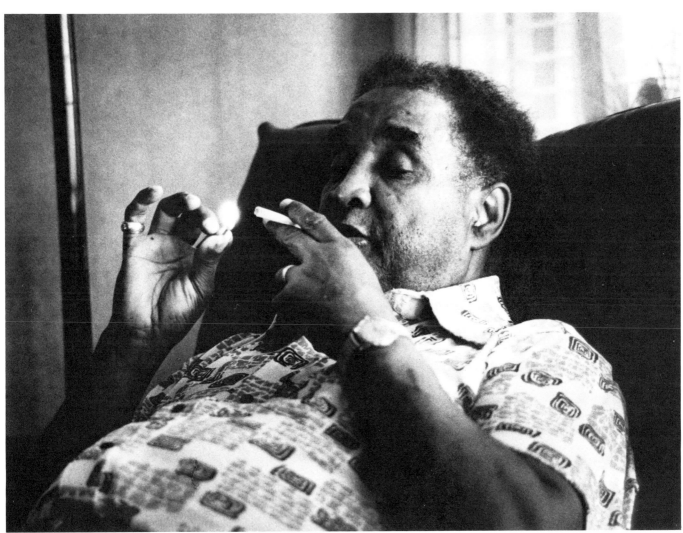

The men just accompanied them. Mamie Smith was the first; Lucille Hegamin was second; Edith Wilson, who was over at my apartment yesterday for a record rehearsal, was third. Then Alberta Hunter. And then it gets on down to Ma Rainey, Ida Cox, and Bessie Smith who was off in a world by herself.

Then there was Lil Green and Chippie Hill and Sarah Martin and Sippie Wallace and Victoria Spivey. Ethel Waters was great back then, too.

Then later on we had this girl Dinah Washington— one of the greats. And Ruth Brown was good at that time, too.

Bessie was the greatest though. When she was singing, no one could touch her. Billie Holliday couldn't touch her. Ethel Waters, Ida Cox, Sippie Wallace, Clara Smith, Trixie Smith—they were great singers but they couldn't reach Bessie.

Son Seals   My father was a musician himself. He was with F. S. Wolcott's Rabbit Foot Minstrel Show for most of his young life. He knew all the oldtimers—Ma Rainey, Red Foxx, a drummer named Fat—and he talked about them quite a bit when I was a kid . . .

He did acts on the stage. He was a good dancer. And he played piano, guitar, drums, blew a slide trombone—he was a heck of a musician.

But he finally settled down in West Memphis and ran a café that had live blues at least on weekends. They finally tore it down, and that's when he moved to Osceola, Arkansas. That's where him and my mother met and got together.

He was forty-eight when I was born, and he'd had it with playing music. He still liked it, though. He had a piano in his café and he owned a big old hollow-body guitar which I fooled with.

But I had it in my mind that I wanted to play drums, so when I was eleven he bought me a set from Memphis. When I was about fifteen I really started getting interested in guitar. I played along with the jukebox and with him on piano.

And when I got to the age that I decided I wanted to form my own group, he provided me with all the instruments I'd need, even though there were ten kids in our family. He realized I was serious, so instead of buying me toys, he bought me the real thing. And I took care of them.

You might say my father put me on the right track, because he taught me everything, right from the start—tuning the guitar, fingering the keyboard. He'd put me on one chord like for *hours*, made me hold it there until it felt good to me. I'd get kind of bored and mad, say, "I'm going outside and play with the kids!" But I learned that he was right: where I wanted to be riffing around all up and down the neck right away, he'd keep me on one chord until I could just feel it in my *sleep*. I'd get up the next morning, reach and grab the neck of the guitar, and I'd be on that chord. So it paid off.

I doubt if I'd've been anywhere at all if I hadn't been surrounded by music on account of him. And I loved it all. As far as music is concerned, I have to owe it all to him.

Luther Johnson—Ellington, Conn., 1974

Luther Johnson   When I was small, it was so rough. There was eleven people in the family. My mother and father was sharecropping on a plantation in Georgia.

I got a guitar when I was six. I had it about two weeks, and a man gypped me out of it at a state fair. My mother whupped me a lot about that. But she got me another one and I kept it, and I been having one ever since.

When I was about thirteen, I found out that the father who was supposed to be my father wasn't *none* of my father. And he was whipping my mother too much. I figured, If I leave, he'll stop doing that, so I ran away from home to Milwaukee.

I didn't know nobody in Milwaukee. I didn't do nothing wrong, but I wouldn't say where I was from, so they put me in reform school for three years. They thought that'd be the best place for me. And I think it was. I was eating something and learning something about life. So I was coming out ahead.

When I was sixteen, I raised my age up and went in the army—started messing around at the Service Club with the guitar. That's where I began to get serious about music.

Junior Wells   Old man Muddy helped me a whole lot, you know. A whole lot of people used to think I was his son.

Luther Johnson   If it wasn't for Muddy Waters, I wouldn't've got where I am today. He told me a lot of things. I was getting mad at him at the time, but I found out later, everything he told me worked out good. He's like a father to me, just like a father to me.

21

James Cotton—Worcester, Mass., 1974

Brownie McGhee The family tree was broken. My mama and daddy separated when I was young. They separated because something was wrong. I don't know *why*. They must've been confused or had the blues, or they'd've never separated. I had polio . . . do you think a mother would've ever left an infant boy in my condition?

I been striving to learn ever since: what happened to mama and papa? Why'd they quit? Was they mentally insane? Was my daddy a cruel man? Was my mother a crooked woman? What happened? They're both dead now, and I'll never know . . .

Hound Dog Taylor I was hurt just once, by my stepdaddy. Never again. I really loved that man. Worked from sunup to sundown picking cotton—you know, cotton's got those burrs that cut your fingers all up—my fingers'd be bleeding—just to hear him say, "You did a good job." But he never did. Never would.

One time he got mad at me. It was Sunday and I was in church with a girl. He came for me; I wasn't doing nothing wrong and I wouldn't go. Next day he came out to the field. I was working in a ditch—the men'd dig ditches and I'd shovel the dirt that fell in—my stepdaddy was on one side of the ditch, I was on the other: I had a shovel, wouldn't let him near me. He was *mad*. When I got home that night he was in the door with a shotgun and a brown paper bag with all my stuff—two little shirts and a pair of pants. He said, "Cut out." My mama was standing right there.

Made up my mind that night nobody'd ever hurt me again. I was nine years old.

James Cotton We used to have this old battery radio that my two older sisters put in their room so when their boyfriends come by they'd have something to entertain them with. They used to listen to things like "Inner Sanctum," "The Lone Ranger" and stuff like that; and I was never into that too much, you know. One day, I just happened to be plucking around there with the radio and I run across station KFFA, Helena, Arkansas, and I heard Sonny Boy Williamson—Rice Miller—play the harp. He had a show there called "King Biscuit Time." And I heard this, you know, and wow!—that sounded *good*. I had a harp my mother had bought me one time for a play toy—something to make noise on. I never knew it was supposed to sound like *that*! And after I heard him play it, I listened to that show every day I guess for a couple of years. Every time I'd get a chance, I'd sit right there by the radio and listen. I learned to play some of his songs—whatever he was playing. I was seven years old then.

My father was a preacher, and my people didn't allow no blues in our house because it was supposed to be sinful music. I used to go way out in the fields to blow blues on my harp . . .

When I was nine years old, I left home which was in Tunica, Mississippi, and went over to Helena, Arkansas . . . told Sonny I come over to play with him. We didn't live too far from there—about a hundred miles across the Delta. So I just split away from home.

I made it to the studio. I'd listened to that studio for two years—KFFA, Helena, Arkansas—and I was *there*! After a while, those cats—the band—drove up in a thirty-four Ford. This was the first day I ever seen

John Lee Hooker and Robert Junior Lockwood—*Ann Arbor Blues and Jazz Festival in Exile,* Windsor, Ontario, 1974

those cats, man. They all had on white overalls, like painters', with the loop down there, where you supposed to hang the hammer, and they had on black caps. I'm sitting there blowing my *mind*! And all of them had on black shirts, man.

So I walked up to the car and said, "Who is Sonny Boy?"

Everybody pointed at everybody else and said, "This is Sonny Boy." "This is Sonny Boy." "This is Sonny Boy."

I tried to give them a hand, help them take their things into the studio. And they wouldn't let me go in the door with them.

When they come back out, I tried to give them a hand again, getting the shit back on the car, you know? And I kept on asking them who was Sonny Boy, and they wouldn't tell me. They drove off and left me there, man.

Next day, I'm sitting right there again. And Sonny Boy finally come up and said, "Hey, *I'm* Sonny Boy."

So I said, "I come up to play with you," and I pulled my harp out of my jeans and blowed him a tune right there.

Well, he went on in and did the show, and when he come back out, he stopped and talked to me. I told him I didn't have no people, which was a lie, and he took me in on the condition that he was gonna find my people; he didn't have time for no kid. But I was kind of a hip cat; I knew what to do. Like they never did have to tell me to do shit. I'd get up and try to help make the beds— stuff like that. And I was always asking questions, you know? He took a liking to me right away.

I knowed all his songs because I'd been listening to him for two years. When I played for him, he said, "I don't know where you come from, but you been listen-ing to me for a long time." That cat couldn't figure me out, man. I knew *all* his tunes.

So I stayed with him about a year and then I told him I had people and where they was, and he taken me back home and met my mother and father and told them I had been with him all the time—playing with him. So they let me go back and play—let me go on doing it. I stayed in his house and played with him for six years.

John Lee Hooker

BOOGIE CHILLEN

Last night I was laying down,
I heard Mama and Papa talking.
I heard Papa tell Mama
to let that boy boogie-woogie,
cause it's in him,
and it's got to come out.

James Cotton   My daughter's thirteen, my son is seven. He's a harp player. And my daughter can do any kind of dance in the book! My son wants to start traveling with me next year. I *might* carry him for a few gigs—let him set there and play a couple of songs and then get him off. See how it goes.

Most of his stuff he picks off my records. When I'm home, he asks me a few things, and I show him. But if I'd been around him more, he'd be right up there . . . His favorite harp player, though, is Junior Wells.

Hound Dog Taylor—Chicago, 1973

Hound Dog Taylor   I got four boys. If any of them gonna be in a gang, I'm gonna kill him. That's *true*. I'm gonna be in jail, he's gonna be dead. I don't want them to come up like me.

Every one of my kids has got a chance. Anything he wants, he will get. Anything he wants to learn is alright with me; anything he wants to make out of himself—a lawyer, a doctor—I be right behind him. Anything he need or want, if I can get it for him, I will *get* it, cause he's got to have something else—brains—behind him.

But if he come around, tell me he's in some kind of gang, if he mess up—unh unh! I'll *kill* him before I'll let him come up like I did.

I went to school just one day—one day, and that was it! I had times when I'd eat garbage off the street. It was *terrible*.

I had to go to work in the fields, so now my manager has to write out my letters for me. If I had an education, I wouldn't need that. I couldn't get a job at Sears and Roebuck right now.

So do you think I want my kids coming up like me? No, I'll kill them first.

Brownie McGhee   I had education on my mind. I graduated in Kingsport, Tennessee—Douglas High—in June, 1936. I didn't finish schooling till I was twenty-one, but I'm not ashamed of it because I did it myself.

I hadn't been operated on yet for my polio, so I couldn't get around too well. And my parents had split. So I lived by myself and supported myself during this time—went to school Monday, Tuesday and Wednesday, and worked the rest of the week.

I used to play my guitar on the street for change, and I worked in my brother-in-law's service station for fifty cents a week, a pack of cigarettes, and three meals a day.

The church deacon built me a little one-room shack on his place, and I went out and picked me up an old stove and an old bed and a heater. They eventually named it "Brownie's Alley." I paid him a dollar and a quarter a week, and I continued to live there for eight more years after I graduated—until I felt the need to hit the road with my guitar.

People think every blues singer is absolutely unlearned, a cornfield guy, but I was just lucky enough to strive for an education. Got my diploma on the wall, baby.

Kennard Johnson   I didn't graduate from high school, man; I didn't have a chance to. Like, I didn't have any choice: I had to either stay in this music and play and be *good* or right now I could be one of the local bums—drinking, talking outa my head, dreaming. Cause there's a lot of them doing that.

I didn't actually go *out* on my own. When I was seventeen my mother *decided* that I should. She gave me the choice: either I go out on my own or stay at home with her and leave music alone. Period. I couldn't do that, man. . . .

I couldn't give up music and I couldn't stay with her, so she decided to move out. I came back home one day and she had moved all the furniture out. I didn't even know where she had moved to. It was really terrible, man. I hate to think about it even now because it really gets me down.

I had it rough, too, cause I didn't have any place to go. It sounds funny now, but we used to get a little group together—about three pieces—and we'd go to different night clubs. Talent money would be twenty-five dollars first prize, fifteen dollars second prize. Shit, if we didn't win any money, man, we didn't eat, so we *had* to go out there and play.

My mother didn't have anything against music. I guess she was just being a mother, you know? She loves me. She loves me now more than ever, I guess because I've succeeded in what I'm doing. She *brags* on me now.

Esther Phillips   Interviewers ask me things like, "What would you be doing if you weren't singing?" Questions like that, I try to be courteous about, but I'm thinking, "Man, how the fuck should I know?"

I look at 'em and say, "What would you be doing if you wasn't *writ*ing?" That's the only way I can handle it. What else can I say? If I'd gone to college, majored in something—even finished high school—I'd have some kind of frame of reference. But I started singing at twelve and now I'm thirty-eight, so how do I *know* what I'd be doing? I might be turning tricks, I don't know. That's a dumb question!

Muddy Waters   I did it all, man. I tried to gamble, and I made and sold whiskey. I didn't stick nobody up but . . . I was successful with my whiskey, though. I used to make that jive out on the Stovall plantation. Had me a little still back out in the bushes, man. I never did believe I could get over working, though, and I probably never would have but for music. I'd've worked to one hundred and five years old and saved ten thousand dollars—*maybe!* Because they wasn't paying nothing. I made just as much as the guy worked five days, seventy-five cents a day. I used to make two-fifty on Saturday night at a frolic or supper with my guitar, and you couldn't make but three-seventy-five for five days' work.

So I laid back and hid from the bossman and made just as much as everyone, and was just as rested as I wanted to be.

You got to use your brain.

Junior Wells—Beverly, Mass., 1974

Junior Wells When I was twelve years old living in Chicago, I remember, I played hookey from school for a week working on a truck in order to get some money to buy me a harmonica. The guy that I worked for didn't give me the two-fifty that I needed; he only gave me a dollar and a half.

And so I went down to a pawnshop on State, and I told the man I wanted to buy a Marine Band harmonica. When he brought it out, he said, "That's two-fifty." I asked him would he let me owe a dollar til the next day, and he said, "No, we don't give credit." Then he showed me another harmonica that he said I could have for a dollar-fifty, but I didn't want that one.

Somebody else came into the store and he went to waiting on them, so I just left the dollar and a half on the counter, took the Marine Band, and walked out. He called the police and they put me in jail.

So when we go to court the man was there, and the judge asked me, did I steal it? I told him, "No, I didn't steal it. I told the man I'd bring in another dollar."

He asked me, "Well, did he give you permission?"
I told him, "No."
So he said, "Don't you consider that stealing?"
I said, "No."
Then he asked me could I play it. I told him, "I think so."
He said, "Let me hear a little bit." And I played it for him.

Then he asked the pawnbroker would it be alright if he gave him the dollar, and the pawnbroker said, "All I want is my money."

So the judge paid the dollar, and he told me, "If you ever get into anything—make a record or something—I want you to make sure I get one." So when I made the "Hoodoo Man" record, I made sure that I gave one to that judge.

Luther Tucker I had to leave Memphis when I was nine. I'd been in lots of trouble—breaking into trains and trailers. The police recommended that I get out of the city, so I went to Chicago to stay with some kinpeople.

Then I got in trouble there—stole a police car. It was just something to do. I loved cars, and my friends dared me. We drove three blocks and I pulled over—pretended to be out of gas. Just then a car came flying around the corner on two wheels. A man jumped out and yelled, "Halt!" He didn't say, "or I'll shoot." Everybody jumped out and started running and he started shooting. Hit one of the fellows in the hip. I got away but they caught up with me.

I spent nine months in St. Charles Reformatory. I was twelve then. It's a very lonely place, and I got ready to run away from there. I was just gonna escape and go anyplace. So I planned it all and then the day came—and that was the day they let me go! I had one of the best records out there, so they let me go early. I'm kind of proud of that. But nine months felt like twenty-one years.

After that my mother said, "Hey, why don't you play music? Do something with yourself? She played piano and guitar, so I picked up the guitar and she showed me the little she knowed.

I was fifteen when I started playing music, and I been playing music ever since.

Outside of Buddy Guy's *Checkerboard Lounge,* Chicago, 1974

Fred Below   Let me tell you something. I was
born in Chicago on the South Side, and I was raised
up in a really rough, tough neighborhood where there
was gangfights, cut-throats, robbing, stealing, dope-
peddling. It was a rough time.

But I knew some musicians—guys like Lester Young
and Johnny Griffin—they pulled up out this neighborhood, and they became alright cats. Some other
guys—lawyers, doctors—came out that same neighborhood. But you had to have *some*thing you could grab
and hold on to, and you did it because you *loved* it, not
just to make a buck.

Carey Bell I was raised in Macon, Mississippi—the hill part. Used to farm.

I decided to blow harp when I was seven or eight years old, and my granddaddy bought my first harp. I couldn't play nothing, but I could always make the notes *end* right; I could just make it end right. The first whole number I learned was "Oh Susanna!" And I went from that to Western and Country music. But when I got a little older I started hearing Little Walter playing harp with Muddy, so I forgot about Western and Country.

I didn't want to farm; I *quit* farming. When I was about thirteen I ran off from the little hometown I was living in and went to Meridian, near the Alabama line. Got a job in a roadhouse washing dishes for fifteen dollars a week. My parents came and found me and brought me back home, but after about two weeks I ran back.

The guy that owned the place, he played guitar and he had a band. They'd be in the front playing on Friday and Saturday nights and I'd be in the back with my dishes. One time they took a break or something and my boss caught me blowing harp. He used to call me "Slick," and he told me, "Hey, Slick, I didn't know you could blow harp. Come on out here." I didn't want to go; so he said, "I won't pay you if you don't." So I went out there, and he said, "Slick, blow your number."

I had never practiced with a band, and I was the only black kid in the place, so I was kinda shaky. It was the first time I ever got on a mike, too, and it sounded real loud. I don't really understand what happened, but when I started playing I got carried away cause the band kept up with *me*. Played with *me*. I wasn't playing with *them*. So that was cool.

All that following week me and him would sit down and rehearse after I finished my work, so I got pretty good at it. That went on for a good while, but somehow they closed the place up and I moved to Texas for a while, then back to Meridian. Got me a job in a sawmill.

I started going around to little joints where they had blues bands. I could blow fairly good by then, and I had some stuff I had made up on my own.

I was outside a club one night listening—had a harp in my pocket—and I started blowing. And some cats went in there and told the clubowner, "Some cat's got a harp." So they told me to come *in* and blow. Three or four guys picked me right up and carried me in there; there wasn't nothing I could do! And it was just like before: they played with *me,* I didn't play with *them!*

I didn't know too much about blues *time* then, so this bandleader did the same thing the other one did: he started rehearsing with me every day. And I started playing blues.

30

Esther Phillips   When I was twelve, living in Watts, I started playing hookey from school, slipping off to the theater—that kind of thing. I was singing and winning in amateur shows, too, but I was scared to give my mother the money.

My sister's older than me, so she could run around when I couldn't, cause I was the baby of the family. One night she and her friend needed some money to buy this white port and lemon juice drink that everyone then was drinking, so she said to me, "Since you like to sing so much, we're gonna take you somewhere that you can sing and make some money." So they dressed me up to look older, which was easy because I'd always been like really developed. At twelve I already looked maybe fourteen.

When they got through with me, they got me in Johnny Otis's nightclub, and I sang a Dinah Washington song, "Baby, Get Lost," which was a hit she had in forty-nine. I won first prize, which was ten dollars. They gave me one, kept nine, took me home, and left. After that, Johnny looked all over Watts for me and tried to find out who I was, but he never found me till later.

Then I started to go to amateur shows at the Largo theater and 103rd Street, where I also went to the movies all the time.

My mother didn't know until one night she came to the theater looking for me, and the man at the door said, "Yeah, she's in there singing."

My mother said, *"Singing?"* So she went in and took a seat, and that night I won twenty-five dollars.

When I got home she told me she'd been there, and I said, "Ohhh my lord!" And the first thing I did was give her the money. After that my mother kind of loosened up a little bit.

Willie Dixon   When I came to Chicago in 1935 I was a boxer—won the Gloves in 1936. I didn't have but three professional fights; I won two and drawed the last one.

I always did like this music thing, too, but the two professions just didn't go together. Because with music you got to be out at night with the gang, and somebody's gonna want you to socialize.

Anyhow, this boy, Leonard Castor—we used to call him "Baby Doo"—he used to come round the gymnasium with his guitar and we'd harmonize; I'd hop over the ropes and sing bass with the gloves on, then go back and box awhile.

Finally, I started going out with Baby Doo, singing at night. And that was the end of boxing.

Carey Bell—Willimantic, Conn., 1974

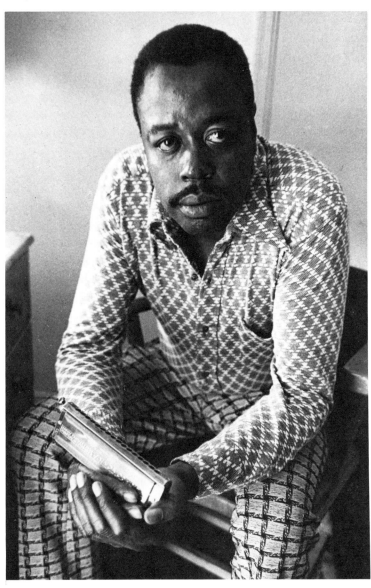

Joe Young One time in Milwaukee when I was on the bandstand, I had to hit a guy. What happened was, he told me he was gonna come, take the guitar outa my hand. I said, "Hey, I'll save you the trouble. I'll pull it off and *give* it to you!" So I pulled it off my neck and laid it on a chair, and I stepped off the bandstand and hit him. It was a surprising blow; he didn't know I was gonna hit him. 'Bout the time he stood up, I hit him again. Straightened him right out.

You don't really want to do these type of things, but what can you do, you know? You run into these wise guys—not always drunk, but they been drinking—and you don't want to wait till the guy swing on *you*. One punch can change your whole fight plan! You don't want to swing too quick, either; you just gotta use your judgment. When you see a guy's going too far, it's just best if you try to be first.

Anyway, I *love* boxing! Joe Louis to me was like Muhammed Ali to the kids today. I liked Sugar Ray, too, and Willie Pep—that cat had brains, didn't he?—and Sandy Sadler. They were something! Oooo boy, they were really something! It's bad to see guys like that go out, you know? But that's life.

I never turned pro or anything, but I tried a little bit of it as an amateur, and I liked it. Had a pretty good punch, too; I could hit pretty hard, you know?

I had one guy that beat me, though. He was too smart for me. He beat me *twice*. So I just went on and gave it up. I figured music was better for me.

Carey Bell The worst thing that ever happened to me was in sixty-six when me and my old lady broke up—my first wife. I'd been married to her since I was seventeen.

At that time I dropped out of music and got a day job for two years.

Then in 1968 when Reverend King was shot, the riots came in Chicago. I was out on Madison Street watching the crowd on the Saturday after the killing. Oh, that street was full of people! But there wasn't a damn thing left there to steal, not after they burnt up every damn thing. So the firemen were fighting fires, and me and about four of five more guys and a bunch of women were standing around. Two squad cars and a paddy wagon pulled up. "Get up against the wall!" So we got against the wall with with our hands up. So I said, "What'd we *do?*" And the cop hit me with his damn gun right on the side of the head. And after that when we were getting in the wagon, I laughed, and he kicked me. I didn't like that.

Well, while I was in jail thinking about things, I got more and more *dis*gusted and blue. Finally, I said, "Forget it! I'll quit my job. Shit. I ain't gonna do a damn thing."

I got out of jail that Easter Sunday, and that Monday I went out to the job and picked up my last pay. Then I went to buy me a gun to kill that cop. I just felt like the whole world had been dropped out from under me.

Then it came to me to go to a music store and buy me some harps. I wasn't gonna *work* anymore, but I could play music. So I bought the harps instead of the gun, and I've been playing music full-time ever since.

Elvin Bishop—*Shaboo Inn,* Mansfield, Conn., 1974

Elvin Bishop   I used to have a real powerful big old radio when I lived in Tulsa, and you could pick up stations from all over the country, you know, late at night when there wasn't much interference. I used to tune in all these different stations and write them down. Then one night I heard this station WLAC from Nashville, which played a lot of blues, and I heard a Jimmy Reed tune and just wigged out.

So the next day I went down to this record store in town that had all the R and B as it was called then—all I knew was that it was Black music—and I stole a bunch of blues records. And I started listening to that station every night and gradually got hip to it. Lightnin' Hopkins and John Lee Hooker were the ones I liked the most, especially John Lee—the emotion of it just carried me away.

At first my ear couldn't handle more than one guy on the guitar, cause I'd never had any musical background; so I dug only the simplest instrumentation. Then I graduated to Muddy Waters and B. B. King and on to jazz.

After I got out of high school, I was lucky—I got a National Merit Scholarship. So I could go to school anywhere I wanted. I didn't care where I went really except that it was a means of getting out of Tulsa. So I chose Chicago. I wrote down on my application either Northwestern or University of Chicago, cause I knew that was where the blues thing was.

And the next fall I went to the University of Chicago.

Bob Riedy   I remember to this day where I first heard real blues—where I was standing and everything. I wandered in to Mother Blue's Club; Otis Rush was playing on a Tuesday night, and watching him was like watching a folk hero. After all my years of imitating music, I was seeing the real thing. He was telling a story, saying exactly what it meant to him and then playing these beautiful riffs behind it. Right then and there I decided that was what I wanted to play. All I had to do was find a way to make it happen.

John Littlejohn   After age six, I was raised up in Jackson, Mississippi, and in the Delta, back and forth, until age sixteen when I left and came to Chicago.

I first heard music at a house party. I loved the guitar, but I didn't have one. But my father did, so I just started "borrowing" it when he wasn't around. My mother'd run me out of the house at all times of the night. And I'd go out on the railroad tracks and sit there and play till I got sleepy and went home to bed.

My daddy didn't know I was using the guitar, until my mother started hollering at me. "I just can't sleep nights. You're just running everybody away from here with your playing." So he come and taken the guitar.

That evening, he tried to talk to me. I just said, "Yas-suh," but wouldn't talk.

A friend of his was there, though, and he said, "Why

don't you let that boy have that guitar? You know how kids is. Some day he might can help you."

So I guess he laid down and thought about it overnight, and he gave me the guitar the next morning. He say, "Now don't lay round here and worry your mother." So I didn't. I used to go out and play by the tracks or by a drainage ditch.

So this is where I learnt a little something about a guitar. I was between nine and ten years old then, and I was coming along pretty good.

A year or so later, my mother and father started giving Saturday night fish fries at the house, selling fish sandwiches and 190 proof corn whiskey . . . my father was a walking whiskey factory. Well, everybody on the plantation would come around to these parties and boogie-woogie all night.

So meantime I was getting better and better on my guitar, learning to use a slide from those old country and western cats, and developing a style *my* way.

We was living in Drew, Mississippi, when I first started playing my country-and-western-type blues for my parents' house parties. I'd play till about two or three o'clock in the morning till I'd be falling asleep. But people'd still want to party, so my parents bought one of those big old nickel jukeboxes and they played that the rest of the night. I'd fall asleep right there with the noise all around me. This went on for years.

And you know, there's something I've thought about many times. My parents made three to four hundred dollars a night, and they never paid me more than a dollar twenty-five for my playing.

Johnny Shines   I'd been hanging around watching [Howlin'] Wolf for a couple of years, and some of his things began to soak in. One Saturday night I was sitting there in a joint watching Wolf and said, "Christ! I can do that!" So Wolf got up and went to take a crap or shoot some craps, and I picked up his guitar and started to play. All his pieces were falling into place. When he come back, I had the joint jumping; he just stood there and looked. So then they went to calling me Little Wolf. They called me Jim String before that. I was Little Wolf for two or three years. I even did a song called "They Call Me Little Wolf."

Matt Murphy—Worcester, Mass., 1974

James Cotton and Matt Murphy—Portchester, N.Y., 1974

Matt Murphy I was a teenager in the late forties when I first started playing with Howlin' Wolf. But Wolf really . . . wasn't playing much at that time as far as I was concerned.

Little Junior Parker and I helped Wolf a lot, because his timing was rather off. While he was playing, a lot of times he would start to *change* at a certain point and I would just cut right on through—keep on playing it *right*. Every once in a while I'd overlook his mistakes and go along but not often, because at that time I was concentrating on *my* time, too, see? Learning about bars—what's four bars? what's two bars? what's two beats? what's a whole rest? I was concentrating on stuff like that, studying these books, see, and that's the reason why I was so critical of Wolf—you know, because I was working to get *my* stuff straight.

While I was playing with Wolf, Junior Parker used to come around and sit in with us. People started liking us together, so they almost *demanded* that we play together. This became a real nice little thing. Junior would play harmonica for an hour or so and then Wolf would take the harmonica. We'd get into contrasting styles: whereas Little Junior was like an idolizer of Roy Brown at that time, doing things like "Corn Bread," boogie things, and shuffles, when it came down to the real low dirty blues, Wolf would take it. That made it really fill out.

I didn't stay with Wolf that long, though, because I was really learning very fast on the guitar and I wanted to venture into other things in music. I was crazy about T-Bone Walker, and I loved jazz. I wanted to go far, go farther, go farther . . . .

John Littlejohn I was working with Wolf at the Council Rock in Chicago. He had Birdbreath on piano—Wolf calls Henry Gray "Birdbreath." I was on guitar—Hubert [Sumlin] had quit him—Jerome [Arnold] on bass. Eddie Shaw on tenor sax, Sam Jones on sax, and Sam Lay the drummer. Wolf got up on the bandstand and said, "This is the best band I've ever had in my life."

But Birdbreath, you know, he like to drink; he started tasting off that bottle. So Wolf say, "Man, I want you to finish the night. I don't want you setting up there getting drunk and all the people looking at you."

Birdbreath say, "Well, I'll just tell you Wolf. I'll just get my shit and go home."

Wolf said, "You can *go* home." And he walked over and unplugged Birdbreath's mike.

So Wolf watched Birdbreath fold his piano up and everything and waited till he got to the door. He had everybody watching. Birdbreath fell when he got near the door cause that piano was heavy. Wolf said into the mike, "Look over yonder y'all. There goes one of my slick new uniform out the door. When he come drifting to me, he was raggedy as a flea-loft. And look at him now, all dressed up nice." Boy, that house went apart laughing.

37

James Cotton—Worcester, Mass., 1974

James Cotton   Sonny Boy used to let me set on his knee on the bandstand. Sometimes I'd play two or three songs a night. Then he'd tell me to go out in the car and go to sleep. And when I'd fuck up, he'd slap the shit out of me and say, "I told you not to do that!"

We'd take turns blowing the harp. Nobody played the blues on harmonica like Sonny did. But we'd take turns. See, down there in the South, we usually mostly worked for the door. Whoever come in give fifty cents when they come in through the door—some places, thirty-five cents. So when Sonny was on the bandstand, I was on the door taking up the money; and when I was on the bandstand, he was on the door taking up the money.

When I was fifteen, we moved out of Helena, Arkansas, up to West Memphis, Arkansas, and he give me his band. He just laid the band on me and said, "Well . . . you make it for yourself." That band consisted of Joe Willie Wilkins, Willie Nix, Willie Love, and a piano player called Five-by-Five.

I didn't even know Sonny was leaving until the night he left. We had never had a drink together, and he never see'd me take one drink of whiskey, cause I had this respect for him, you know? And he walked up with this half-pint of whiskey and made me sit down and drink it. After we set down and drank it, he said, "Well, I'm planning to split. The band is yours. You can make it for yourself now."

Me being young, and everyone else in the band was older than I was—the band kind of went to my head. I got wild right away, and the band just fell apart.

I thought I was a star. I really thought I was a star!

All of a sudden, I found myself standing up front with Sonny Boy's band behind me. I'm standing there, fifteen years old, man; I went *crazy*. I screwed up *every*thing!

I just did everything wrong. They couldn't tell me nothing no more. When Sonny Boy stepped down, he gave the chicks a better chance to get a look at me; I never had that before, and it really screwed up my mind. I started getting drunk, half showing up, everything I thought a star was supposed to do. I knowed I was a star, man! The cat done give me the band, what'd you expect; I just knowed I was *there*. I wouldn't let them talk to me. I thought I knowed everything. Those guys had been playing as long as I was old, and every time they tried to tell me, they couldn't tell me *noth*ing. So they finally just left, finally just cut me loose . . . because I was *crazy*. I don't blame them.

After that, man, everything fell off. I suffered for a while. I got a job driving a dump truck, hauling gravel. I had some time to realize what had happened . . .

Sonny Terry   I was in Wadesboro, North Carolina, in 1934, when I first met Blind Boy Fuller. I used to go up there on Fridays and Saturdays and make me a little money for the next week, maybe seven or eight dollars.

I was playing one side of the street and he was playing on the other. But I heard this whining, wailing guitar, so I told a little boy, "Go tell that guy playing the guitar to come over here." While that boy was crossing the street, Fuller sent someone over to get *me!*

So I went over there in the middle of the afternoon, and we played til round about seven or eight o'clock in the evening. We fit together pretty good, and he told me, "Come to Durham, North Carolina. We can maybe make a record together."

We played and recorded together for about four or five years after that—until his bad kidneys killed him.

James Cotton— Worcester, Mass., 1974

Hammie Nixon   We was begging for food back in 1931 when times was really hard. I remember one time when [Sleepy] John [Estes] said, "I'll tell you what I just thought about. You work that side of the street; I'll work this side. I'm gonna be blind, deaf, and dumb."

I was gonna be just regular begging and keeping a watch on him.

So I watched him knock on a lady's door. I could hear the whole thing good: he said, "Whoo, whoo, whoo, whoo."

She said, "Lord, this poor man is deaf and dumb and blind. I don't know what this poor man wants." Then she said, "I know! This man must be asking for bread."

So the lady went to get some bread. She left the door open and forgot about her little old feisty rat terrier. Well, John always was scared of dogs. you know. So that little bob-tailed terrier jumped out that door and started nibbling on John's ankles. Round the house, round the house, they ran—John yelling, "Whoo! Whoo! Whoo!" Finally he yelled, "Lady, get your god-damned dog off me!"

He ain't said that "Whoo! Whoo!" no more since.

Willie Dixon   I was raised in Vicksburg, [Mississippi]. I almost never saw my old man.

My mother made two dollars a week, and rent and everybody's food had to come out of that. So I would go out with other kids in the city and hunt junk after school—find pots and pans in the alleys and in garbage cans, and pieces of brass down in the bayous—and sell it. The money would buy us each a meal, and that was the last food we'd see till the next day.

When I was about fourteen I got put in jail for stealing some stuff out of an empty house. I was guilty.

Me and two other boys, we had our sacks, and we went to this empty house—a White person owned it. The house had bathroom fixtures with copper linings, and we pulled them off and took them down to the junkyard and sold them for about sixty cents. The junkman told who we were, and we got a year on the county farm, called "the Ballground."

They made a waterboy out of me, and I worked at the bossman's house. We called him "the Captain," and I didn't like him because I was afraid of him. When he said go do this, go do that, I ran and done it. I would cook and wash dishes and milk the cow and work around the house. And at noon I would bring the Captain his dinner, wherever he was. I got off two months early for good behavior.

There was guys getting beaten—you could hear them hollering. I saw guys beaten for nothing. And I would run back to the house because I was scared.

I wanted to get completely out of Mississippi after my experience at the Ballground, so when I got out I left for Chicago. And on my way, farther north in Mississippi, I was arrested for hoboing. They didn't *catch* me hoboing, but I did ride the train up. But I jumped off the train outside the yard and started walking around the city, and a man said, "You get off that train?"

"What train?"

"Yeah, you got off that train. Come with me." I didn't have a chance to say anything. Man, they'd catch *any-body* walking along there. The people that lived there knew better, I guess.

So they took me to the Harvey Allen Country Farm, near Clarksdale. When I arrived, a guy said, "Man, you got thirty days." That guy was police, judge, jury, and jailer, all in one.

If they didn't like you on the farm, they'd do anything. I never saw anybody beaten to death, but I heard of it many times, and I saw plenty of coffins around. I learned to keep the hell out of people's way. I spent all my time trying to duck and dodge everybody. And after two weeks I cut out.

Prisoners would say, "Hey, look, man, the inspectors is coming today. Let's tell them about what's going on!" They didn't realize they'd only be telling the same people that *put* them there. Nothing was gonna change. They may have these things going on today but we ain't gonna hear about it. They keep things pretty secret.

There was nobody there who was a criminal. They was all victims of circumstance. Just folks. . . .

Lightnin' Hopkins

LONG GONE LIKE A TURKEY THROUGH THE CORN

Ooh looka here, ooh I see that red-eyed captain there.
boys he's coming after me.
I'm long gone like a turkey through the corn,
long gone like a turkey through the corn,
long gone with my long pajamas on.

Lightnin' Hopkins—New York City, 1974

Sonny Terry   The FBI come to my house and said, "Sonny Terry, we heard you was a Communist."

I say, "What in the hell is that?"

They say, "Don't be funny."

I say, "Funny, hell! What is it? You say I'm *that;* now what is it?"

They say, "We won't say you's the devil until you say you signed up."

I say, "I ain't signed up with shit! I don't even know what it is."

They say, "Trying to throw the government."

I say, "Shit! The goddamn Japs couldn't throw them. How the hell can I?"

Willie Dixon   Things are still pretty bad in Mississippi for Black folks. I was in my hometown of Vicksburg just recently with Buster Benton, and my relatives advised me, "Don't go back up to Memphis the Delta way, up Highway 61, even though it's fastest. Go over to Jackson and up from there." Cause in the Delta when they see your nice big car with Black faces in it and Illinois license plates, they start hassling you and might even throw you in jail. So we went one hundred miles out of our way to be safe.

Other areas are just as bad. One night Otis Rush, Little Brother [Montgomery] and I were driving away from a job in Florida. We were doing about fifty miles an hour, and we were stopped for speeding. Well, the speed limit was sixty. They took us to the judge. "I'm gonna have to put you boys under a bond of one hundred dollars apiece. Come back day after tomorrow." We had a schedule: we were supposed to be in Tennessee then. So we made a call to the booking agent. When we finished, the judge said, "You called your boss man. Well, he ain't *no* one around here." And he raised the bond another one hundred dollars apiece.

Man, the word "justice" is a joke!

Willie Dixon—Chicago, 1973

Robert Junior Lockwood and family—Cleveland, Ohio, 1973

Robert Junior Lockwood—Cleveland, Ohio, 1973

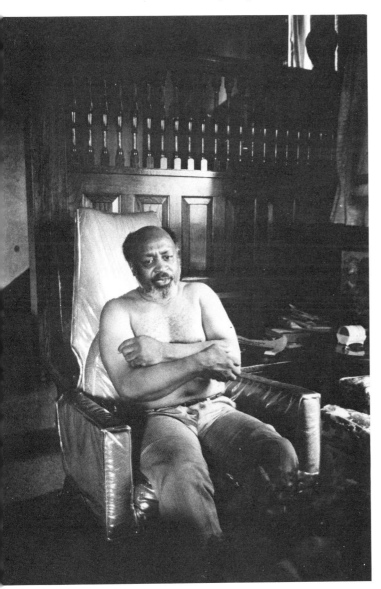

Robert Junior Lockwood   Back in the 1940s before I had a group, I played at a plantation in Mississippi one time and got my stuff chopped up. My guitar and amplifier, mike, and stand got chopped up with an ax.

The owner had told the men on his plantation to stop having parties and I guess he felt that if he chopped it up, the man I was playing for would have to pay for it. So he hired some dude to do it. That dude's a lucky man. When I found a man's shotgun hanging on a rack over the door, he was out of sight. Otherwise, I'd have blown his fucking brains out.

I was in my thirties then. It was in Mississippi. I think I'd had the equipment about six months. I got it from Montgomery Ward and I was only paying eleven dollars a month, so when he cut it up, I went to Montgomery Ward, told them about it. It didn't cost me a damn thing but the down payment. The down payment was nothing. My mother had an account with Montgomery Ward. I just went and told them if you're not going to help me . . . it's your merchandise as much as it is mine. It was cut up, it wasn't no accident, it was purposely destroyed, so somebody's going to pay for it. So we just dropped it. So I just went out and got me some more stuff. Bought some stuff from Montgomery Ward since then—they don't even mention it. I don't know if that man paid for it or not.

Sonny Terry   We went to Baltimore in the forties with Woody Guthrie to do a concert down there for a union. After the concert they had a big dinner for us. They had all the big tables set up, all the food and everything, and we walked in with Woody. And they say, "No. We can't serve *them* in here." Baltimore was a Jim Crow motherfucker then, boy.

Woody say, "You mean, goddamnit, you can't serve these boys in here after they played for you all this evening? And now we can't eat together?"

They say, "No. We can't serve them here."

Woody told us to meet him out front in a few minutes, so we left. Then he tore that place *up,* turned every table over. Food all over the floor. Then he said, "You goddamn sons of bitches can pay for all this yourselves. If we can't eat, *no*body's gonna eat!"

Yeah, Woody was an all-right cat.

Esther Phillips   You know how old I was when I discovered I was Black? You won't believe this: I was nine. My mother and I had moved from Houston to Los Angeles when I was five, but we lived in Watts, so I still didn't have that contact with Whites.

But then I went back to Houston to live with my father, and my sister picked me up at the train station. And like all kids, you know, I wanted the window seat. So I get on the bus, and I jump right behind the driver. And my sister says, "You can't sit there."

I said, "Why?"

She said, "You just can't sit there, Esther."

And then as I was walking toward the back, I saw a big sign on the exit door that said "Colored," which meant that we had a few little seats in the back and all the seats in the front were for Whites. And all of a sudden, it just fell into place. My sister didn't have to say any more about it.

Sonny Terry and Brownie McGhee—*Shaboo Inn,* Mansfield, Conn., 1974

Joe Carter—*South Park Lounge*, Chicago, 1974

Johnny Shines Any time someone wants to call me "nigger," I give him the privilege, because only a Nigger could have subdued and gone through the things that we, the Black people, have gone through and survived. So if you call me "Nigger," you only identify me as one of the strongest in the world. I feel like it's an honor, not a disgrace to be called "Nigger." To me it tells me I am the strongest. Only me and a beast of burden—such as an ox—could have subdued and survived. Anything else would have been extinct by now.

Willie Dixon The Black man in America knows he's just like the rabbit. He's the victim for every damn thing that comes along. The fox is looking for him; the wolf is looking for him; the Man is looking for him. Everybody keeps him on the run to survive.

Honeyboy Edwards In 1942, in Mississippi, I done this thing for Allan Lomax, for the Library of Congress. I was young, and I was playing good then.

He came looking for me one Monday morning. I don't know why or how he heard of me, but he did. I was living with a woman out in the country. She was old enough for my mama, but I was living with her.

Anyway, he came there in a brand new Hudson, and when Annie came to the door he said to her, "I'm looking for a boy they call 'Honeyboy.' He play guitar."

Well, you know how people in the country are; she was scared to say anything to a White man cause he might do something *to* me, so she said, "I don't know."

He said, "I'm from D. C., the Library of Congress, and I'm looking for him cause I want him to do some recording for me."

So I told her to tell him to come on in. We talked, and then we went to Clarksdale and rented a motel room out on the highway. And then we went to a school outside Clarksdale, and that's where he recorded me—in a big colored school. They had to stop the recording right in the middle cause a big storm came up. That was "Worried Life Blues." We did about fifteen others, but "Worried Life Blues" is the one that got all the talk about it.

I never made any money off this thing, but it sure helped me getting jobs.

Brownie McGhee   The talent scout that picked me up was a Black boy that heard me playing on the streets of Burlington, North Carolina—J. B. Long. He said to me, "I think you're doing something strange and good. I want you to sing a song tomorrow on the telephone to a man in San Francisco." That was *his* head boss at Okeh Records.

So the next day he called his boss and said, "I want you to hear this guy."

I was listening; The man on the other end said, "What, you got some more garbage?"

Anyway, I sang "Me and My Dog" for him. That was my first song, and it was nothing but a poem I'd written and put to blues. It was about a girl that had left me in my little shack, left me and my dog there, and that's all I had for companionship for quite a few months. She left her clothes there, and looking at those clothes and this dog every night, I could almost have become an alcoholic.

I could tell on the phone the man didn't want me, but J. B. Long told him, "Listen, he's got quality. And I'm gonna bring him up *myself*." So he took me to Chicago to make some songs.

He asked me, "How many you got?"

I said, "Any amount you want."

I didn't make but a hundred and twenty-five dollars for that session, but that seemed like wonderful pay for just singing. A hundred and twenty-five dollars for nine songs! I was used to playing nine songs for a couple of bucks.

And I just kept doing it. I didn't know the record business, so I signed anything he put out; I signed myself away! I signed all my royalties to him. He's even got his name on some of my early songs.

If I'd had money and knowledge, he'd never got his hands on me. But I didn't have this, so Okeh Records wouldn't deal with me. I was green, I was ignorant, and they don't want to be bothered with stupidity. So instead they deal with the man that knows talent and say, "He's your artist." It was years before I learned that I wasn't under contract to Okeh. I was J. B. Long's artist; he was paying me and taking the rest.

But I signed myself onto a stepping stone, too; it was a good deal for me. And he *deserved* something. I think it was just fair. A lot of entertainers have never understood that it takes money to make money and that somebody's got to in*vest* in you. What J. B. Long got was just what he was entitled to.

So he never did me any injustice. He was a marvelous man, and I have great esteem for him. I always honor J. B. Long. I give respect to J. B. Long.

Big Mama Thornton—*Brooklyn Academy of Music,* Brooklyn, N.Y., 1974

Pinetop Perkins   Around 1933 I was playing by my-self in Mississippi and singing—oh, man, I could sing like a bird, yeah!—and this cat told me, "You play too much like Memphis Slim. You get a style of your own, you'll make it." So that's what I did.

So after a while this sport came around to where I was playing and saw me by the name of Robert Nighthawk. He liked the way I played, told me, "Look here, I need you in my band." I didn't want to leave where I was working without giving any notice, so Robert went on over to Helena, Arkansas, and I joined him two weeks later on the Bright Star Flour program on station KFFA.

Every day for Bright Star we came on around twelve-thirty in the afternoon, played thirty minutes. The biggest thing that did was advertise the band. People would hear us, they'd want us to play for them. They'd write the station and get us, and we'd go differ-ent places—all over Mississippi, all over Arkansas. That's how we made our living.

Then the Interstate Grocery man heard me. He told Sonny Boy Williamson—he was playing on the King Biscuit program on KFFA—"That sounds *good!*" Hah! So Sonny Boy told me about it, and I switched over to King Biscuit. Robert Nighthawk hated to see me go . . .

We'd go on the air at twelve-fifteen every day, and then we'd get out there, sell Sonny Boy Meal, King Biscuit Flour. We used to go out touring on trucks, played on trucks. Oh, I liked that life pretty good!

Big Mama Thornton   I started traveling in 1939, when I was fourteen.

God bless the dead, Sammy Green had a show called "The Hot Harlem Review" out of Atlanta, Georgia. I had won first prize on an amateur show, and he was looking for a singer. So I started traveling with him.

I was singing, dancing, doing comedy—I still use a little bit of that now—and all I was doing was *go*ing—through Alabama and Georgia and back to Alabama; I kept coming home to Montgomery, Alabama.

In 1948 I quit the "Hot Harlem Review" because they owed me quite a bit of money. They wouldn't pay me, so I went to Houston, Texas, and got me a job at the Eldorado Club.

In 1951 I did my first hit tune, called "Let Your Tears Fall, Baby," a blues song. It made a good hit around Houston. That kept me going through Texas and all down in Louisiana.

When I come back home to Houston, I worked with

Roy Milton, Joe Ligon, Joe Ligon's brother, and several other bands. I got the name "Big Mama Thornton" when I was with the Johnny Otis show, in the fifties. Before that I was billed as Bessie Smith's younger sister.

Anyway, in 1953, when "Hound Dog" broke loose for me, that's when I met Johnny Ace. I worked on his show up to 1954 when he decided he didn't want to be in the world no more; I *guess* that's what he decided, cause he blew his brains out.

I always had self-respect. I was responsible for looking after myself because I was on my own. I saved my pennies. And I always held my head high.

Brownie McGhee   I took the road with my guitar—went off to the coalfields in Virginia, Ohio, West Virginia—just walking. That was after my polio operation, and the doctor said, "Now Brownie, you can go out in the world and seek your future. Play your guitar without stopping." I didn't need my crutch and cane no more, and I got that wandering mind. I was proud to have my operation, get rid of those sticks.

I played in the coalfields, and they gave out scrip instead of money. But I had a deal with the man. He'd give me cash for scrip provided I play at his commissary.

So I played in quite a few mining towns and didn't mind getting paid off in scrip. Always had a few bucks in my pocket.

Whole lotta *Black* miners, baby, and that's why I survived. I played blues for them and country music for the Whites.

Honeyboy Edwards   I been all over the Delta and out to Texas and different places too—Oklahoma, New Orleans.

I was young and got a lot of kick out of being on the road and I met a lot of pretty girls. Made a lot of money, too, but I spent it up as fast as I got it. Cadillacs and clothes—you got to make a good appearance. Blew it as fast as I could make it.

Yeah, I've played a lot of places and I know a lot of musicians, so many of them, it's a crying shame. Some recorded and some didn't. Lots of them was good, ain't never done nothing, cause they was stuck back in the woods or on the farm and never had a chance.

I met all these musicians, cause I never *stayed* nowhere. I'd meet a different musician every week. Sometimes I'd stay with them three or four days, get acquainted, then cut out. Go meet some more musicians. Cause quite naturally, all musicians want to meet each other and learn from each other, just like preachers.

So I kept on moving. There was never any telling where I'd stop at. I'd get tired of some place, be down in Louisiana the next week; get lonesome, be out in Texas two days later; get broke, just up and go two or three hundred miles.

Pinetop Perkins   When we're traveling, we eat Kentucky Fried Chicken a lot—we call it "The Colonel's." It's pretty good when it's hot. And we like to find us some beans and peas and greens—soul food.

When we get a place to stay that has a stove, we cook for ourselves. Muddy—he can cook anything. Bo, the chauffeur, cooks sometimes. I can cook, too, when I feel like it—greens and ham hocks and stuff like that.

Man, oh man, get me some milk! It's *good!*

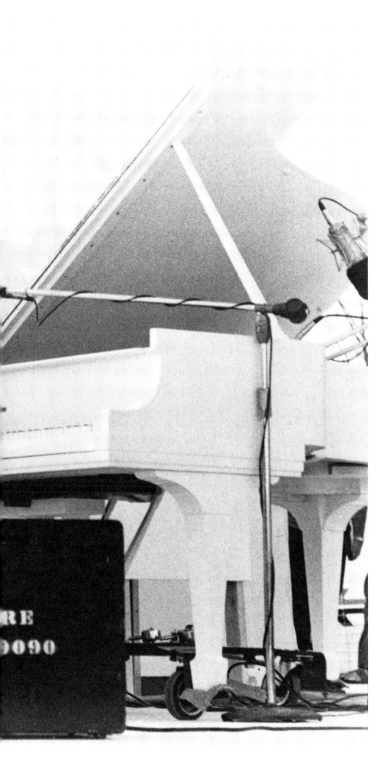

Roosevelt Sykes—*Ann Arbor Blues and Jazz Festival,* Ann Arbor, Mich., 1973

Roosevelt Sykes   I came to Chicago for no special reason when I was quite young—just wandering. I did a lot of things without any reason, just *go.* At that time I had nobody crying about me where I just left, nobody expecting me where I was going. So I mean I was a happy man. No family or nothing. Hoboing.

  After thirty-seven years, I left Chicago for no certain reason. Since then, just call me "international." Everywhere. I'm just a guy that likes to move around. Any place where there's a piano's home to me. I go overseas, don't be knowing nobody. Don't know the language. I point at what I want to eat. Never had any trouble. I was just blessed.

Johnny Shines   Robert [Johnson] and I played together a lot—traveled to Chicago, Texas, New York, Canada, Kentucky, Indiana. I tagged along with him cause I knew he was heavy and I wanted to learn.

It was pretty rough at times; we didn't know where the next food was coming from or where we'd stay that night. Robert and I would travel *any*where to play and make some money. We'd hear about a sawmill going to pay off at a certain time, and we'd be there; we'd pick up maybe seven dollars just playing where the payday was. And then some guy might hire us to play somewhere for four dollars a night and all we could drink. Different guys'd give us a quarter to play this piece or that piece, so we'd end up with twenty-five or thirty dollars.

Everything was fun in those days, though, cause you wasn't taking much of anything too serious. You'd wake up with a couple of black eyes, lip all swollen up and a loose tooth:

"Man, you sure kicked that son of a bitch around last night!"

"Shit, look like to me he kicked *my* ass!"

Sometimes I'd get the worst of something Robert started. I've had guys stomp my intestines so I felt like I'd been stomped by a mule!

The thing about him—if women pull at a musician, naturally men's gonna be jealous of it. Because every man wants to be king. I say that with authority: *every* man wants to be king! And if he's not king and somebody else seems to be on the throne, then he wants to get him down. It don't take very much to set people off when you're being worshipped by women. And so naturally we got into a hell of a lot of trouble.

He never talked about himself or bragged nothing, and he was peculiar, too; you never knew what he'd do next. Like one evening we played together and he took off right in the middle of while we were playing, and I didn't see him for weeks. He was quiet most of the time—until he started drinking. Then he was like anybody else—rowdy!

And I never saw him reading or writing. Robert didn't have any education at all, I believe; he was a *nat*ural genius. Robert just was born to sing and play the blues . . .

Honeyboy Edwards   I remember Rube Lacey came down to Greenwood in 1931, right after he recorded "Hambone Gravy" up North—'bout how he got to get his hambone 'fore it spoils. He was playing at a Friday night party at a man's house, and we all gathered up there and danced and drank whiskey and gambled for nickels and dimes. Well, there was so many people, they broke right through the floor. That's right—caved it in! And when he left, he carried that man's wife back with him, a pretty Creole woman with long hair on her shoulders.

You know, a musician back forty or fifty years ago in the South had a lot of women. The women be pulling all over him, giving him drinks—but there was men wanted to kill him!

Men was jealous of musicians down South there in the country. Some men was crazy about their wives—had them good-looking wives, go to dances. And they thought because you was a musician, you might take those women away with you. Cause you could do something they *couldn't* do, they was jealous of you.

A lot of times, you maybe just wanted to be friends. You didn't want every woman, and every woman didn't want you. But the men didn't see that. They hated musicians on account of women.

I got hurt once or twice like that. One time in the Delta, a man thought I was talking to his wife—said, "That little old boy there, he think because he play a pretty little freckled guitar, he's *some*thing." Then he chunked a coke bottle right at me and hit me!

Big Mama Thornton   I had a hard way to go when I come up. Sometimes had to go to somebody's back door and ask for bread or something cool to drink. "Mister, could I have a drink of your water?" Sometimes they said no. I just kept on walking.

I just made myself happy. People didn't know I was worried a lot of times. I always kept a smile on my face: I always be round friends, buy drinks, laugh. But they didn't know what was going through my mind.

A lot of times, man, I didn't have nothing to eat. They didn't know it. I was smiling. Didn't have nowhere to stay. They didn't know that. I slept in all-night restaurants and barrooms.

Course it don't make no difference now. It's all the past. Anyway, I couldn't *express* what I went through. It don't make no sense to people today.

Honeyboy Edwards   I was nineteen years old in thirty-four—just getting pretty good—when Charlie Patton died. He was only around forty-one then, but he was all cut up from being such a hell raiser. His neck was cut, too, which hurt his singing in the end. His voice staggered some when he sang; you can hear it on his last recordings.

I remember I came through Holly Ridge Plantation. It was on a Monday, I think. I had my guitar on my shoulder, walking down this little old gravel road.

So I saw a fresh grave by the road. Little country graveyard. Big trees. Black clotty gumbo mud on the grave. A little wreath on it.

I stopped in a little store to get me a pop, and the boy there said, "Did you know Charlie died last week?"

That grave was Charlie Patton's grave.

Pinetop Perkins—*Shaboo Inn,* Mansfield, Conn., 1973

Pinetop Perkins We was drinking whiskey in the back of a place called the Dreamland Cafe in Helena, Arkansas, and this girl come back there. And you know how women be at the end of the month? She was bleeding like a hog—you know what I mean? She went and heisted up in the toilet—didn't shut the door. Finally I looked around and seen her, and I shoved the door to: told myself, you know, I was helping her out. And her husband Leroy—I'll never forget his name—put about three barrels of dad-blasted ashes up to the door—cinders and stuff, you know—so's she couldn't get out. I didn't know it, cause I had walked out and I was standing up at the front, talking.

She come over to me and said, "I want to see somebody who shut the door!" Then she just started whacking at me with one of them little knives . . . didn't ask me nothing, just went to cutting me. What she did, she started at my heart and I put my arm up so she hit my arm; cut all that stuff loose in there—the muscle, all the ligaments. For nothing! I didn't do nothing but shut the door to her, trying to help. That's where I got that scar, twenty years ago.

It still cuts me down on my piano playing: I used to have my basses rolling like thunder, man.

Gatemouth Brown Blues works in many ways, happy and sad. It can do a lot of strange things to the human mind. I've seen the form of blues that can cause death. If you play those blues all night at a dance where there's a lot of booze in the house, you'll have fights. I mean the real low backwoods blues that's based on hardship. You sing, "My Mama Messing with Another Man." Some guy in the audience living that life, he gets up. Gets mad. Gets violent. His wife may be dancing with another man. You got a killing on your hands. I seen that happen many times.

I had a very hot song, "Have You Ever Been Mistreated?" Cat gave me five dollars to play it. I remember he had on old bib overalls and some gator shoes. During the song, I heard four shots. We thought at first it was a firecracker, till all of a sudden, this guy came running to the bandstand, his eyes looking like glass. He ran back to the door and fell like a bird on the banister and slid down the stairs to the ground outside. By that time, we was through playing. We was running for the door along with everybody else in the place. The cat with the gun walked down the steps, kicked the dead man in the ribs, and left. That was in Silsbee, Texas, in the forties.

Another incident I saw happened in Mississippi. A Delta-style guitar player named Joe was playing the blues; a woman came up and threw a can of potash in his face. I think it was because he was playing that lowdown Mississippi music. It's like a preacher, especially a Negro preacher. I seen them work on the emotions. Before long, that whole place is hysterical. T-Bone Walker was a good example. I seen so many fights at his dances . . .

58

Gatemouth Brown—New York City, 1973

Hound Dog Taylor This White woman and my sister was friends, and she kept on coming over to where I was playing at house parties and stuff. And I'd be setting there looking, you know. God-dog! So we got together.

At that time a White man could be with your woman, you know, and you'd be out on your porch. But you couldn't say *nothing;* you better not come in there till he be through—he would get a mob and *kill* you!

So this jealous colored girl went to the White girl's husband and told her about us. She didn't *see* it, she just told him what she *thought.* And this cat took her word for it. He was right about us alright, but he still don't have proof. He don't *know* today! He just made a fool out of his own self!

He came to my house with a rifle, and he found me on the porch with a gun of my own. If he'd've lifted his gun he'd've been *gone.* So he turned around and walked away. I heard he beat the shit out of his woman with a stick, but she wouldn't tell him nothing.

All my relatives running around, telling me I had to leave. It wasn't no lie! Shit, they was gonna hang my ass! Finally, I said, "I'll see you all later."

I was sitting out back behind a stump. I think there was fifty men out there that night with flashlights, shotguns, rifles, hound dogs, all around the house. I wasn't scared. Hell, I was looking for it! A guy passed a few feet away from me: if he'd discovered me behind the stump there would've been so many dead it'd be a crying shame! But he turned around and went back. I just made sure nobody bothered my sister, and when they all moved on I walked about five miles down a gravel road and stayed the night with a friend of mine. He took me to a bus the next morning and I got away from there.

Willie Smith My family was farming outside Helena, Arkansas: planting cotton, chopping cotton, Picking cotton—we was *do*ing it! I picked quite a bit and drove tractor, all that kind of stuff. Driving a tractor was fun, but picking and chopping hurt my heart. And I remember telling my uncle one day—it started raining—"I wasn't cut out for this."

He laughed and said, "What else you know?"

I said, "I'll *find* something else!"

So when I was seventeen, I left there for a two-week vacation to visit my mother in Chicago. That was a two-week vacation that's lasted twenty years.

Muddy Waters My manager wants me to buy some ground down in Arkansas, but he don't really understand . . . I don't want to go to Arkansas. He's buying a place down in Missouri or Arkansas—Missouri, I think. He's buying some ground, and he's telling me how beautiful it's gonna be, and it's gonna be worth something. But I don't want no ground, man. This is something new to him. He never been on a plantation and dug any of it. I was raised in Mississippi . . . I don't want to be digging in no ground.

60

Honeyboy Edwards I knew Little Walter when he was just a kid, about fifteen. He was married at that time, you know. Married a girl twenty-five years old named Pearl Lee from Helena, Arkansas. Walter and I met in St. Louis and decided to get on up to Chicago.

So we left East St. Louis in 1945, walking on Route 66. We'd walk awhile, flag a ride, walk awhile. Walter had on some canvas shoes till he wore them out. Wasn't nothing on the bottom after a few days.

So we came into Chicago and stopped in Jewtown. Started playing over there on Maxwell Street on a Sunday morning. We filled our cigar box up with coins about three times.

Walter had a sound that didn't nobody else have, even though his harp was old and broken and only had two bass notes. He could play them with as good a punch as when he was recording later.

So we played that Sunday, and I guess we made about thirty dollars apiece. Met some pretty girls, too.

A lady came by that Sunday. She was a sanctified woman—a religious woman. But she liked what Walter and me was playing and she liked Walter, and she dropped a note down in the cigar box. The note told him to come out to her house and gave the address.

So Walter went out there that Monday, and he didn't come back till Tuesday. She had dressed him up—suit of clothes, shoes, new shirt. He come down on Maxwell Street as sharp as he could be! That's right!

So I stayed with Walter all that summer and I left him around the first of September. I went back South. Walter stayed on in Chicago, and later that year he met Muddy.

Carey Bell Honeyboy [Edwards] introduced me to Little Walter—said to me one day, "Hey, you ever meet Little Walter?" I said no, so we goes over where he was playing and sat in.

And Little Walter says, "You blow pretty nice harp. I'd like to show you a few things." So the following week I go over there by myself, and the manager wouldn't let me in because I was underage. Walter told him, "Well, I don't play if you don't let him in."

"Well," the manager says, "You gotta take him on the bandstand and be responsible for him."

"Damn right. Come on."

So we went up to the bandstand and he got to playing "Juke." "Can you blow that song?" When I said no, he told me, "You gonna play it tonight!" And he played about two twelve-bar solos and turned it over to me. And, man, that was sickening! I didn't know if I was playing it right or not!

Intermission time he says, "Come on, let's go out. You drink?"

"Yeah."

"What you drink?"

"Don't make no difference." And he had wine, whiskey, and gin in the trunk of his car.

"Can you play third position?"

"No." So he showed me. He'd do it, pass the harp to me, I'd try, pass the harp back—

"You're gonna do it or *whup* me," he told me.

I said, "*Ohhhh* ohhhh!" I had heard a lot of talk about him. And then that cat *slapped* me—boy, I could see stars! So I'm thinking, "I'm in it now. I got to blow this harp right or he's gonna *kill* me!" So I finally got it. It was the first time I learned third position, and now I do it every night.

A lot of guys say Walter was hard to get along with.

Amateur singers—*604 Lounge,* Chicago, 1974

But not to me. He gave me money, bought me clothes—I would go to the Salvation Army where you could get shirts for fifteen cents, sport coats for a dollar and a quarter. And I was always sharp and clean. I lived with Little Walter for almost a year—had a lot of fun with him. Or I should say, he had a lot of fun with *me.* I never had no trouble with him. No more than the time he slapped me. But maybe if he hadn't slapped me I wouldn't be playing now.

Luther Tucker   I played with Little Walter seven and a half years, from 1952 to 1960. When I first started playing with him, right after he made "Juke," we had to go to the union to get a permit for him to take care of me when I was in the clubs, cause I was only fifteen.

I'm on all his records, and we worked clubs as a band. The Aces was with him at first, but later it was Fred Below on drums and Robert Junior Lockwood and me on guitar. It was a pretty heavy band. We *al*ways got an encore. It was an amazing thing what that cat could do with a harmonica. We used to be on the bandstand, and people would come up and open up his hand to see what he had in there to make that beautiful sound. I can remember, too, we used to jam with sax players, and each note they blew, Walter could turn it around. That cat could do something with a harp no one else since has done—play five positions on one harmonica. I don't even think Cotton could do it.

He was a beautiful cat to work for, although he was kind of wild, and sometimes he didn't want to pay the band right. We disputed over money, and that's why we left him, one-by-one: first Below, then Robert Junior, and then me.

After that he had trouble getting somebody to work with him, because he didn't want to pay the right bread. I wouldn't say he started going down be*cause* we left him, but right after that he did start going down . . .

That cat was wild, too—loved to smoke grass, drink whiskey, chase women, fight—I been with him lots of times when there was a fight. Walter and I worked to*gether.* He'd say, "Okay, when I hit this dude, you put your foot to him." Walter slaps the fellow, knocks him down. He turns to me and says, "Come on, Tucker!"

I say, "Man, you almost kilt him! You don't need no help!" He was tough and strong. But there's always somebody a little bit stronger.

And he beat women, too. If a woman give him some lip, he'd fatten it up for her. And they'd just love it. I couldn't understand it myself, but that's the way it was. It was amazing; they liked what he was doing! He just had a style all his own; he really got over.

I wasn't in town when Walter died, but I have a pretty good idea what happened. I think it was because of a woman. I heard Walter had a knife and gave it to one of his friends and told him to go outside of the club and back him up. So the fellow took the knife and stood there ready, outside. When Walter came out, the other guy hit him right off and knocked him down, and his head hit the sidewalk. Then he had a terrible headache, so he took some aspirins and went to bed. I heard he never woke up.

Ted Harvey   I was setting up late one night after work in a nightclub on the South Side. A young lady and I were getting us a nightcap. I always keep my pistol in the back of the car, and I figured I'd leave it there this time of night, 3:00 A.M. "I don't need it."

All of a sudden, here come about ten young hoodlums pushing in the door at one time. And they started a hassle in the front. I knew the bartender, and he ducked in the back room. Well, I knew what he was going for, and I asked my girl to slip out and get my gun. Them guys was raising a boatload of sand in the middle of the floor, trying to stir something up.

When the young lady got back with my gun, the bartender was back with his. I said, "When you're ready, I am." I had the gun on the bar under my cap. I'm facing these guys, and he's behind me—real serious.

These kids began to realize that this club wasn't going to be no pushover . . .They'll come into a club, take your beer, and go to drinking it; and if you say something, pow! you'll have three or four on you . . . But they knew this place was ready, and they eased on out the door.

Elvin Bishop   We used to have great times down there at Pepper's Lounge on Forty-third Street. They had a stand out front that sold pig ear sandwiches. They're nothing but gristle and bone—put a lot of hot sauce on them and they taste real good when you're drunk. I was in there one night when I was at the University of Chicago and I took this girl, this really kind of proper college girl. I took her down there, said, "Come on, I want you to see this." She was digging the music: Muddy Waters was up there playing. But then there was this faggot waiter down in the front who had a fight with his boyfriend and pulled out a gun and started shooting.

The next thing I knew I was two blocks away, leaning against a building puffing. I had completely forgotten about the girl.

Luther Tucker   We'd be playing in Chicago and our lives'd be in danger. One night at the old Pepper's on Forty-third Street—I was with the James Cotton Blues Band at the time—we come out to the street to catch a breath of fresh air between sets. I'm standing on the corner; I looks around. Here's a dude on his knees with both hands on a pistol pointed right at me! I say, "Man, be cool. Shucks." I'd never even *seen* the cat before, and he was ready to blow me away! He was out of his head!

I just couldn't handle all the meanness coming down there. It didn't make no sense. So I moved on.

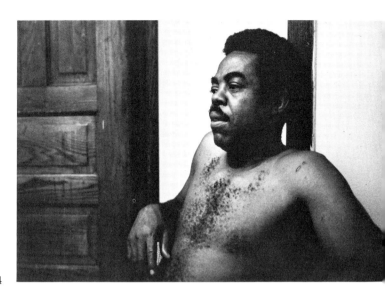

Sammy Lawhorn—Chicago, 1974

Hound Dog Taylor   About three years ago they ripped me off over there on the West Side in Chicago. It was in the hallway, coming out of a highrise; two men grabbed me. The taller one wanted to hurt me but the little short one said, "No, man, forget it."

You see, a thing like that—you're not looking for it. Maybe you been drinking or something. Anyway, you're not looking for it.

So they took everything—my pants, my wallet, my shoes. I don't know why they took my clothes. Maybe they didn't have nothing to wear, and I had on good stuff. I wrapped up in a coat to go home—no shoes on— and the snow was *deep*. The police passed me in a car, and they *laughed*—didn't do nothing. Now, if the police see somebody with no clothes on in the middle of the night, they're supposed to do *some*thing. Gotta be *nuts* not to do anything . . .

Sammy Lawhorn   I had just finished a gig down South with Muddy [Waters] and flew into Chicago.

As I was getting to my apartment—it was *late*— these robbers was coming out of the apartment across the hall. I was just putting my key in the door.

They grabbed me and pushed me into my apartment and knocked me down. Then they kicked my teeth out and broke my nose with brass knuckles—tried to make me tell where some more money was, which I didn't have. A couple of them were so full of dope it was a crying shame.

Then I found out the one with the gun really wanted to shoot me. He kept on begging the others, but they said, "Don't shoot him now. Wait till we get through; then shoot him."

Then I started hooking them right and left, but three of them just got me and went straight into my bathroom with me, and threw me out the window. I didn't have any time to think. I just had time to try to make a turn in the air, and I made a half-turn. If I landed like they threw me, I'd've landed on my head. Instead I just broke both ankles and both legs. That's why I always sit down on the bandstand.

Hound Dog Taylor You can have about five guys with you, or you can have your heat with you—understand? Somebody asks you, "Hey, man, you got a cigarette?"

"Naw, I ain't got a cigarette."

"You sup*posed* to have a cigarette. You been around this world a long time, had it good all that time, you sup*posed* to have a cigarette."

Then you got a hassle. But you say, "No, man, I ain't got a cigarette, You want to *take* one?"

They say, "He ain't got no cigarette, Come on, man, let's go." Hah hah—you ain't got *no* problem! If you give them a cigarette, then they want something else; they want a quarter. They keep on till they got their hassle going.

The best thing is stay *out* of those neighborhoods if you possibly can!

Luther Allison From five until thirteen I had a beautiful life down in Mayflower, Arkansas. I had good grades in school, and I was in one play at the age of about ten. I loved that acting part; I *loved* it. And I loved the South.

Then I got into Chicago, and I see all these kids running around—the whole thing of fighting. From the age of, I'll say, twelve to twenty-one, it's rough for kids in Chicago. It's *rough.* You might go to school and not return, it's that bad. Some kids, they got the knives, twenty-two revolvers and whatever. It's sad. Why do a kid gotta be throwing rocks and breaking windows and fighting and stuff?

I managed to come up in Chicago with only one fight. Hey, you know, I got beat simply because I didn't know I already had the guy beat. Anyway, I was one of the lucky ones. I didn't want to fight.

66

Carey Bell   My stepdaddy was Lovey Lee and I was in his band. He came to Chicago first and he stayed two weeks. When he came back home he said, "Man, we going to Chicago!"

I said, "What we going up there for?"

And he said, "I seen *every*body—Little Walter, Muddy Waters, Jimmy Rogers—and everybody's playing, making good money."

"Okay!" I had about three, four hundred dollars saved, so we all jumped on the bus, the whole band— five of us—and came to Chicago.

The first job we got was where Jimmy Rogers was working. He had to go on the road so we got a chance to get his gig. We was making eighteen dollars a man, and I had never made that much money in my life. I was thinking I'd get me a Cadillac! Only two weeks working and I'm gonna buy a Cadillac! After two weeks we were out of work again, and I had to spend all my money.

I didn't know the city. I didn't like to go nowhere by myself and I didn't have nobody to take me looking for work, so it took me a good while to get a job. And the whole band was living all piled up in a little kitchenette.

Then I got lucky. One of the guys in the building worked in a carwash. He took me there and I got hired. I was the only guy in the band working, and they would go out to find gigs, and sometimes I couldn't even play on 'em because I had to get up early for work.

But I got a better job later in a wastepaper company. The money was the same, but I didn't have to work weekends, so I could play with the band. So that put me right back in music.

Sonny Terry   When me and Brownie [McGhee] first come to New York in 1940, we lived for about seven or eight months in an old big house on Sixth Avenue with about twenty-five or thirty people. Pete Seeger, me, Brownie, Woody Guthrie, a guy named Gordon, Bessie Lomax, Cisco Houston, a schoolteacher named Nick, and a whole lot more stayed there. Pete handled all the organizing.

We'd get up in the morning: we didn't have enough money to buy no bacon. We'd pool our few little dollars together and go out and buy a great big old loaf of bread and about two or three dozen eggs, which we'd scramble up, and fix a pot of coffee, and everybody eat like hell.

We played music together every night, and every Monday we'd have a "Blue Monday" jam with Burl Ives and Josh White and his friends. Bessie's brother Alan used to come down a lot, too.

Then on weekends everybody'd go out and play a little—they called them hootenannies then; now we call them concerts. That way we'd make a little change, but we never had much.

We all started out from that, and everybody started doing better as time went by.

Jimmy Dawkins and band—*Ann Arbor Blues and Jazz Festival in Exile,* Windsor, Ontario, 1974

Jimmy Dawkins Back in my first years in Chicago, I was working a factory job and trying to play a little at night. We'd get off work and go up and rehearse on the corner of Roosevelt and Albany, right out on the sidewalk. They wasn't used to live street music in that neighborhood, see, so we had the corner sewed up. Quite a crowd came and tossed money into the drums.

But there was a problem with this tavern across the street. The people there couldn't play the jukebox for all the noise, and we couldn't hear what we was doing for his noise. So there was always a confusion.

Finally, the tavern owner said, "Come in my place, and I'll cut this damn jukebox off until you get through making your noise." And he even gave the four of us ten dollars apiece a night to rehearse in his club.

Buster Benton When I was first living in Chicago, I was a car mechanic, but I was learning my guitar and studying my music, too.

I used to go around Buddy Guy and Junior Wells and get up and play with them. My timing was very bad; my singing was good but I couldn't back it up with my guitar. The crowd would like it—be patting their hands—but the musicians knew; they'd be back there laughing at me. I was going through what every young bluesman goes through, but I was doing it in *pub*lic.

So I disappeared for about three months and stayed on my guitar all the time, every day—playing along with records like B. B. King and Albert King—and avoiding people. I wouldn't be *seen.*

During that time I met Joe Young. I didn't let him know I was trying to play guitar. What I would do—I'd get close to the bandstand, and every time he came down off the bandstand I would buy him a drink and be talking to him about different things—but never too much about the guitar. But I watched him real close.

And then I came back out, and I've been out ever since, full-time in music.

(Left) Lonnie Brooks—Chicago, 1974
(Below) B. B. King and Gatemouth Brown—New York City, 1973

Lonnie Brooks I've seen a lot of blues battles; I've battled in a few, too. Me and Buddy Guy battled week after week when we were playing out on Madison in Chicago, till I beat him three straight times, and he quit. And I remember a guitar battle on Sixty-third Street where the audience applause gave it to King Edward. They said I was clowning too much, doing tricks with my guitar, so they disqualified me. A lot of the crowd got mad and left.

The *greatest* guitar battle I ever saw, though, was in 1955, in Port Arthur, Texas—Gatemouth Brown, who is my granddaddy in blues—the one who made me want to play—and B. B. King, who had just made a big hit with "Please Love Me." B. B. was bigger at the time, but the audience went by who *played* better, and they gave it to Gate. Two thousand fans!

That Gate can do more with a guitar than a monkey with a peanut!

69

Luther Allison   My first, my very first, getting into lead guitar was by playing with B. B. King's record of "Whole Lotta Lovin'." An hour before school in the morning and an hour after school. Me and that guitar made a lot of people hate me. I had a little amplifier about the size of a wastebasket on my back porch. And every day I just had to tickle a tune until I finally got it to sound like B. sound. Then I went a little further, started listening to Otis Rush, who's another very unique guitar player. He's clear, but he's difficult because he's lefthanded. And then Freddy King, Magic Sam . . .

My advice to young musicians would be, first of all, you go to the library, you dig up some Robert Johnson music that's been written, that somebody done wrote the notes to it.

Second, pick up some simple Jimmy Reed records. He'll show you that solid electric blues pattern.

Third, play your own leads to him.

Fourth, listen to a lot of B. B. King because he's smooth. He's so clear, you can hear what he's doing. And study it, just study it . . .

Joe Young   A young dude wants to get a record out, wants to get his talent around. So he takes chances.

He don't know all the background of a company or what they got in their mind or all the things they can do—how they take tunes and slick you out of them, and give you old, fouled-up contracts. The only thing he's looking out for is his career, and he wants to get a record out and get his name out there. So he records. And there you are.

If he starts acting like he's too smart or knows too much, he can forget it. They ain't got the time for him anymore.

Joe Young—*Charlie's Place*, Cambridge, Mass., 1974

Calvin Jones (guitar) and Willie Smith (drums)—*Shaboo Inn*, Mansfield, Conn., 1973

Freddie King   When I was just a kid, I would sit there and I would listen to these guys—these musicians—talking about how a guy cheated him out of money and stuff, and I wouldn't say a word. I would just sit there and look from one to the other, and I would think, "I ain't gonna let these cats do *me* like that once I get started." I was looking out for all this, so nobody never cheat me too much; I was *schooled* by all them.

It used to be, you know—you a blues singer, you Black, the record company buy you a Cadillac and that's *it*. That's right! Then you owe for that Cadillac for the rest of your life. As long as you stay with that company, you never do finish paying for it.

But, see, when I first went to King Records, I already *had* one; I drove it up there and recorded! So—Cadillacs didn't really *excite* me.

Bo Diddley   My mother hipped me to something early: she told me, "Son, go down there to Chess Records and borrow some money. And ask for more than you want. Get some advances, cause they're liable to go broke or bankrupt or anything." So I went down and borrowed a grand—put eight hundred in the bank, and blew the rest.

She hipped me good, you understand, cause that's what happened finally—Chess did sell out and left a lot of cats hanging.

Brownie McGhee   See, I was versatile enough to change from one style to another, even from one instrument to another. So I took these other recording jobs even though I never made much money off them. It was *quick* money, and I had a family to support.

I'm Big Tom Collins on one label. I'm Henry Johnson on Decca. I'm Blind Boy Williams on Jade. I played piano on that, and my brother [Sticks McGhee] played guitar. And of course I was Blind Boy Fuller Number Two.

In fact, "The Death of Blind Boy Fuller" was my biggest blues record. Quite naturally, people wanted to see the man who made the tune, cause Blind Boy was a big name in the South. So they sent me on a tour.

J. B. Long gave me Blind Boy's guitar and three hundred dollars for expenses. I put the money in my hip pocket, felt like a king, and hitchhiked around the tour—didn't even buy no food. I went all through South Carolina, North Carolina . . .

People were looking for me to be blind, you know, cause J. B. Long tied on me the name "Blind Boy Fuller Number Two"; that was promotion for the tour. Then I found out "Brownie McGhee" was in small letters, "Blind Boy Fuller Number Two" was in *big* letters, which my daddy was horrified over. He raised hell about it. "Son, he's de*stroy*ing you!"

I said, "I know who I am." And after the tour I came back to Brownie McGhee.

Willie Smith I always had a dream of playing blues.
My favorite bluesmen was Blind Boy Fuller, Louis Jordan, Lonnie Johnson, and all those guys. Those was my
main *main* men. I wanted to play like Louis Jordan,
but I couldn't afford the horn, so I got the next best
thing—a harmonica.

I was doing alright with the harp, but as you know,
the blues went completely dry at one point around the
end of the 1950's and harps went out. So I had to look
for other ways to keep a job, so I learned drums.

Then blues got even slower. You couldn't get nowhere with blues unless you was real famous. Even
Muddy [Waters] couldn't get work. Even B. B. [King]
wasn't getting the work. He used to have almost an
orchestra, you know; and it got so bad, he had to cut
down to three or four pieces. It got so bad, to be honest
with you, I finally quit in sixty-four and took a job
driving a cab for a few years.

Bo Diddley You gotta change. You gotta come up
with a gimmick to stay out here. There's maybe five or
six songs—the first ones I recorded—that I don't get
tired of. A lot of the other stuff—I don't even want to
play it. Because it's discontinued—you can't even buy
it—so why should I play it for the kids? I've already
been paid for that.

A lot of cats come up and say, "I'm one of your old
fans and blah blah blah."

And the first thing I say is, "You have a *new* album?"

And he says, "Uh—yeah, I got one; I got the *London
Sessions*."

I say, "No, you ain't got the new one. There's about
six albums since, then." That told me he stopped
buying albums back where *Bo Diddley in London*
stopped at. So I figure he's there to listen, and I'm way
ahead of him. So I'm sorry, I just lost that one. Cause
I'm after the new ones now.

I watched them. The kids have put up with so much
of that old stuff, and they get tired because there ain't
nothing happening. That stuff is finished. If I did "I'm a
Man" all over again, I'd fall flat on my face. Back then,
in that era, that's what was happening.

But in order to get to the kids of today, I got to bend a
little and step it up. This is one of the things a lot of
entertainers refuse to do. And that's why you don't
hear them no more. I've got a few little tricks up my
sleeve—things people ain't never heard me play before.
I don't know how it's gonna click. But the whole thing
is to change, man.

And when I get so old I gotta have somebody to tell
me how to play my axe and what to do with it, that's
when I hang that sapsucker up.

John Lee Hooker with the Billy Colwell Band—*Shaboo Inn,* Mansfield, Conn., 1973

John Lee Hooker   In those clubs in the north, you *had* to play electric—otherwise no one could hear you. But I got to love those electric sounds I could make.

When I'm playing with a band I don't play a lot of guitar—not like I would if I was by myself. With a band I mostly care that the rhythm have a really good, driving beat. A *boogie* beat. Nowadays the kids like something with a big beat, and you gotta do what these kids want. But when I'm playing by myself or in a small combo, I can play more guitar and get more *into* it.

I love coffeehouses, but there isn't as much money as there is playing for concerts or clubs. About five or six years ago—maybe a little longer—I played mostly coffeehouses. I played with David Clayton Thomas—you heard of him? He's with Blood, Sweat and Tears. We used to play with two guitars—me and him—and a little guy named Eddie Kirkland. Finally this thing got so big—concerts and colleges and dancehalls—I decided to get a band. I made a little switch there. I had to go with the kids and go with the money. You got to survive.

Doctor John   Cats like John Lee Hooker and Lightnin' Hopkins can play them folk clubs with an acoustic guitar and get them off. People look at them and say, " 'Well, look at that old man. That's all he know.' " But go down to their own stomping grounds like in Texas somewhere. They'll set up an electric guitar and scare the shit out of you.

74

Bo Diddley   It's written in a book I played guitar for Muddy Waters. Nobody ever asked *me* about that, and it's a lie. Some writers put down just whatever they want; I don't think that's very cool.

I was not even up to his standard. Muddy was *way* advanced over me. There wouldn't've been no way I'd even been able to au*dit*ion for Muddy, because I knew nothing about nothing at that time, and Muddy was the Godfather of the Blues around Chicago. I didn't know but two songs!

Muddy has been some of my inspiration cause I wanted to be so much like him. But I couldn't even begin to think about being the man he is in the blues bag. Muddy is the greatest.

I wasn't even what you'd call a blues artist. I was put into the R and B lineup because they didn't know what the hell to call me, man. Finally, Alan Freed started calling me 'Rock and Roll.' It was a new sound—rocking and rolling. And then Freed titled me "a new sound in Boston" at the Lowell State Theater. I was the first one—almost a year before Elvis was even thought about.

So at seventeen, eighteen years old, I became a "threat" to Muddy Waters, because I was raising hell around Chicago with my little juke band, you know? And I couldn't play but two tunes!

Muddy Waters   I was a disc jockey for about six or eight months on WOPA in Chicago. You notice how I talk—I don't talk too good—but I was getting over, man. Peoples was having fun with me up there.

I used to talk so much they'd call and tell me to quit cutting in on the records. One guy called me, said, "I wish you'd get off the air and quit *bull*shitting!"

So I just cracked right back, "Some stupid dude just called and asked me to get off the air, and he ain't got brains enough to get *on* the air! And I'm sitting here looking at my pretty white Cadillac." Oh, I come on strong. Man, I was scared to go home that night.

I was disc-jockeying under Big Bill Hill—he was a good blues man, too—and I was playing strictly blues. Sometimes a cat would call and say, "Why don't you play some *music,* man? Get off them blues. How about some jazz?"

And I'd say, "All you have to do is just turn your radio dial a *lee*tle bit and you can miss me."

I'd tell audiences who was playing where in town. I'd say, "I'll be there about ten o'clock," and the place'd be *jammed.* And I hollered so much on the air I'd be hoarse that night. Oh, I carried on terrible!

One day this record guy, I can't call his name—Bobbie Blue Bland recorded for him; still does, I think—was at the station delivering some new records to Big Bill Hill. He asked me to mention his name, and he give me fifty dollars to do it. Boy, I hollered *some,* then! He sent me all his new releases after that.

When it got so's it was taking too much out of me, I quit; I was just doing it for the hell of it, anyway . . .

Mojo Buford   I came to Chicago when I was twenty-six in 1953, and we formed a little trio called "the Savage Boys." We played after hours parties and got thrown in jail and all this. And then Bro Mud—I call Muddy Waters "Bro Mud"—got wind of us from Otis Spann, and he started advertising us on WOPA where he was a disc jockey. And then he took us as his junior band, and when he'd go out of town we'd take over his gigs. I'm the original Muddy Waters Junior. And I was thrilled a few years later when he asked me to come with his band.

Bob Riedy   In 1968 I was broke, had no band, and had no equipment. I needed bread first. So I got a day gig sweeping floors in a poster shop. Eventually I became manager—till we got robbed and burned out. But I worked for two years and saved enough money for a piano. During those years I was borrowing an old upright and learning. Every night I'd go home after work and listen to Otis Spann and Ray Charles records, playing them over and over, and slowing them down to catch the tricky parts. Well, after I got my piano, I got a group together and went looking for gigs. But no one wanted to hear anything about blues.

So finally I said to the Wise Fools people in Chicago, "Let me come in with my group and we'll take the door and I'll put out all the posters and everything." I called it rock, but I invited Johnny Young to do one set in front. He was the first bluesman I'd gotten together with, and he needed work as badly as we did. In fact, no one in blues was working much at that time, even Muddy.

So anyway, I brought Johnny Young in to front the rock group, and it was exciting—a novelty. As long as

Bob Riedy—Chicago, 1974

Big Mojo Elem—*Crystal Lake Ballroom,* Ellington, Conn., 1974

we didn't call it blues, it was cool. Then I started changing members in the group. I started realizing through Johnny Young that all these guys I'd been listening to on Otis Spann's albums—see, Otis Spann was dead by that time—were still alive. So I got Louis Myers on lead, and Louis introduced me to his brother Dave on bass, and Dave brought Fred Below on drums, and then Johnny Young told me about Big Walter, and pretty soon we had a whole black blues band. And me.

We worked together regularly for over a year, but things started happening. Johnny Young and Big Walter started fighting every night. At first it was okay; they didn't get too drunk. But then they'd get drunker, and drunker, and drunker, and they'd be physically fighting over the mike. And the owner would start getting a little shaky about that. So I traded off. I couldn't keep Johnny off a gig. He'd be on my doorstep, afraid I might go to a gig without him. But I tried to work it out where I'd have Johnny sometimes and Big Walter other times. But not at the same time.

Then I started getting troubles with Fred Below and Louis Myers. They demanded more money than we were even making and I finally had to let them go. That's when I got a hold of Jimmy Rogers, and John Littlejohn, and S. P. Leary on drums. Which was fantastic, cause like playing with S. P. was like playing with half of an Otis Spann album. So with S. P. I could play twice as good; and it was *great!* I was listening to

albums during the day, and coming to the gig at night. It was fantastic. I was just eating it up as fast as I could, putting those posters out there to make sure people would keep coming through the door. Anyway, then we started having Sunday things with Big Walter and Johnny Young, periodically. Then we started having a jam on Sundays—finding out that more and more bluesman were still alive and out of work. We'd have Muddy Waters come up. James Cotton. In fact, I put together shows with Muddy Waters, Howlin' Wolf, Buddy Guy, Junior Wells, Hound Dog Taylor—everybody. I even put together Muddy's old group with James Cotton, Jimmy Rogers, S. P. Leary. And people wouldn't come across the street for them. That's how popular blues was in Chicago.

Then I began figuring that all our eggs were in one basket. If something happened to Wise Fools, the whole thing would be dead again and we'd be back to straight day gigs again. So I went downtown knocking on every door I could, every agent, and they wouldn't have any. I wrote letters and knocked on doors, but nothing was working. So I went to a newly opened club called "Alice's" and talked them into giving my band a gig. I didn't want to lose the Wise Fools. So I booked in someone else. And that's the first time I booked another dude.

Now, I spend nine-tenths of my time on that kind of business and one-tenth on playing, when I'd like it to be the other way around. But that's what I've got to do to survive and play the kind of music I love. If the blues scene here on the North Side of Chicago goes down the drain, I go down, too.

Elvin Bishop I played in three or four different little bands with Paul Butterfield before he got up the Butterfield Blues Band. We had a little trio with James Cotton and made some tapes, which, incidentally, Cotton tells me he listened to recently and liked. Basically, we were learning how to play. When I first met Butterfield, all he could play were Sonny Terry licks and then he went on to Jimmy Reed, and then little Walter and so forth, until he finally graduated to his own stuff. This was about 1960 when I met him, and he could play guitar better than he could harmonica.

We used to go down and jam at all the joints on the South Side. We picked up gigs. Maybe Magic Sam or somebody would offer Butterfield ten dollars a night to play harp with him for a week, and he'd do it. I played with Junior Wells, played with Hound Dog Taylor, played with J. T. Brown—all kinds of guys. I didn't make a lot of money, but it was a big encouragement being able to walk down the street and say, "Hey man, I'm gigging with Junior Wells this week." I'd put on my continental suit. I'd be *slick!*

Finally, we put a band together and we started playing this place called Big John's on the North Side of Chicago. It was a half-White and half-Black band, and it was the first time that any kind of blues band had played on the North Side of Chicago which is the white part. For some reason it just caught on immediately, fantastically. We did six or seven sets a night for six nights a week, for two years straight; and the joint was always packed, people dancing on tables and stuff. I

guess they got wind of it in New York, and this guy named Paul Rothchild from Electra Records came and signed us. We didn't get no front money or anything. We just went in the studio and in about three days we cut twenty-five or thirty tunes. They victimized us. It was the old way of treating artists. You go in to cut an album, and what you really want to do is cut *one* really good album. But you end up giving the record company twenty-five tunes. They come out later, and you don't get any session checks for them. *I* ain't seen the money from those cuts. It wasn't really that big a rip-off; it's just that we could get a better deal now. You look at a band that was as influential as Butterfield's was, I mean that really busted a lot of things open, and the rewards that he's seen out of it are pretty slim.

The original band was Sam Lay, Jerome Arnold, Butterfield and myself. Then we added Mike Bloomfield, and then Mark Naftalin.

Bloomfield, incidentally, was about the only other white guy besides Butterfield and myself that I used to see in the South Side clubs at that time. He used to hang out down there all the time with Big Joe Williams.

Bob Riedy   I'm a musician. I'm not an agent. I don't *want* to be an agent. All I do is whatever needs to be done, but I do end up spending most of my time on business.

The gigs I book are bread-and-butter gigs. And the only time I ever do any booking for a man is when someone else hasn't been doing his job; it's as simple as that.

Basically, I try to get up a two-month schedule of live blues at five North Side clubs—groups that I know will show up on time and do a good job. There are a thousand problems, and one of them is jive bluesmen. First off, there are way too many good bluesmen for the money and gigs available. Beyond that, there are about thirty jive artists for every bluesman who is legitimate. So that's why I try to book groups like Otis Rush, Sam Lay, J. B. Hutto, Son Seals, Jimmy Dawkins, "Blueblood" MacMahon, Magic Slim, who are gonna be dependable. This is important because a lot of these clubowners are very easy to alienate. So it's very important for me to earn their trust.

Sometimes I wonder why I got involved in all this. But I've been through it all, up and down, and I recognize that there's no choice. If I wasn't doing this, we wouldn't be playing. And I can see an overall plan to it. The main thing is, I can play exactly what I *want* to play. I remember in the days I was playing top forty on the road—I hated to go to work, dreaded *play*ing. And I love the music I play. I love blues.

Brownie McGhee   In 1942, I started a place in New York called "Home of the Blues"—got a charter from Albany and had my cards printed up—where I just tried to help young artists develop what was in them. If you come to me with an idea for a song, I didn't want your idea, I wanted to help you relieve yourself of that burden. If you thought you had a song in mind, I wanted to know *why*—what created it? People'd come in with some beautiful ideas, and I'd help them express it in writing, and then I'd secure a copyright for them, help them sell it, record it for them, book them, see that they got paid.

It only cost a dollar to join, and then you paid for whatever services you wanted: guitar lessons, piano lessons, voice, stage presence, mike technique—whatever you wanted.

I had Blind Gary Davis teaching guitar—he was an extraordinary teacher; and I had a white Jewish boy from Long Island teaching Country and Western; and then I had a real fast jazz guitar player for people who wanted that. We had a little recording machine and made acetates for people.

I gave it up in 1950 because I got married and my first baby was born and I needed to make some money. So I got back out there in the entertainment world. Besides, I was tired of that desk and telephone and cigar.

Brownie McGhee with fan—*Shaboo Inn,* Mansfield, Conn., 1974

Buddy Guy   I got a club on Forty-third Street—The Checkerboard Lounge. One of the main reasons I got my club was that Theresa's was about the only place left on the South Side to have blues. All the other places, now, feature soul stuff; they don't even know who Junior [Wells] and I *is* now.

It didn't cost me that much to open; it's not a fabulous club. Sometimes—most of the time—I get kind of disappointed with it, but I knew it was gonna be hard because it's hard to get good help and get the place run right when I'm not there to watch over it. But I don't really look for the club to *do* anything . . .

I play there as less as I can, and I get criticized for that. This gets me kind of disgusted—everyone looking for me to be there and play. But I don't feel a very heavy responsibility, because it ain't making me that kind of money. Besides, I didn't buy the club for Buddy to play at; I bought it for the local cats to do like I was doing before I got a chance.

Hound Dog and Cotton and different people comes in and plays. Not that I can afford to pay them much. They just come in and sit in like we did in the early sixties at Theresa's. I didn't make much money there either, but I had a lot of fun.

James Cotton   I'm trying to accumulate a few bucks because someday I want to get my own club—maybe in Boston or Memphis, *not* Chicago—and just call it James Cotton's Place. I'd have a whole lot of good entertainment there because every club has to be noted for something—good food, good drink, good music, or *something*.

I would treat the musicians right: make them feel at home, pay them a good price. And do you know where their dressing room would be? Right back of the bandstand. I wouldn't make any musicians go out into the street all sweaty.

Two nights a week—Monday and Tuesday—I would like my main attraction to be all the local talent around the city. You got to give the local boys a chance, too.

A club the size I'm thinking about couldn't book B. B. King, but he could drop in when he had a night off and see his friends. This means a lot to a musician—to see smiling faces that you know. I'd like to have a club where you would walk in, see B. B. King over at the bar, see Muddy Waters setting down the other end with some friends, Big Joe Williams in the middle. . . .

There ain't a blues musician across the country that I can't call at home. I don't need to talk to his agent. I'm his *friend*. And if an artist couldn't bring his own band, then me and my band could back him.

James Cotton and Muddy Waters—*Paul's Mall,* Boston, 1973

Muddy Waters   I got some growing musicians out here in my band. They got their own mind. If I push them too hard, they ain't gonna play good. You should leave them *loose*. Like you let a bunch of cows loose in a pasture, say, "Go get you some grass."

Now, the average man in the band is not too crazy about the boss anyway. They may love him in some ways, but they're not too crazy about him in other ways. I try not to get upset when they complain. They don't know the years I come through to make the name, so I let them say things—just tuck my tail and walk away.

I've talked about this with [James] Cotton. I used to tell him, "Wait till you get out there on your own; you'll discover the headaches." He's said to me a hundred times since, "Baby, you told me the *truth*."

James Cotton   I had a little better chance than the average bandleader has: I was raised *up* with a bandleader [Sonny Boy Williamson], and he showed me what to do. Then I come in and played with Muddy twelve years. I see the right things he did, I see the wrong things he did; I see what should've been did and what shouldn't've been did. All I learned from Sonny Boy and Muddy—that stayed with me. So I know pretty well what is supposed to go on, you know?

In any group of five or six people, there're gonna be different ideas of how things should be done. The problem is trying to get them to go down the road together. And that's where I come in. This is *my* job. Sometimes I got to be nice, sometimes I got to be tough.

I don't mess with their personal life or tell them how to live. As long as they show up for work and do a good job, I'm happy. I fine any musician that gets drunk on my stage. After the show, that's his business.

They are my family. I don't be nobody's father, but any organization has to have a leader. Like when it gets cold and geese fly south, they got one goose out there in front; they *all* got to believe he's flying the right way . . .

James Cotton Band—*Shaboo Inn,* Mansfield, Conn., 1973

George Smith—*Academy of Music,* New York City, 1973

George "Harmonica" Smith   As a sideman you don't make much. You just *go.* The person says he'll give you one hundred dollars. You got to pay your room, expenses, your eats out of that. So you got nothing to take home. And this is embarrassing to me, because I done it so much.

My kids, they come up to me. "Hey, old man, where you going?"

"I'm going to Buffalo." Or, "I'm going here, I'm going there."

"Well, okay, you do a lot of going. But . . . I know you gonna come home broke."

And it hurts me, because that's just what I'm *gonna* do.

Doctor John   Man, it was a comic book world when I was coming up. There was all the time fights and stuff. Many was the night when we'd be going to do a session and another session would be breaking up and there'd be a fight in the alley—somebody didn't get the money for the date and he'd be kicking somebody's ass in the alley right outside the studio.

Sometimes we'd agree to do a session for ten dollars a man, and the dude would say, when the session was over, "Well, I'm gonna give you five dollars cash and straighten you for the rest tomorrow," knowing we were leaving town that night. Right off there was a fight.

That was a day-by-day survival thing for money, cause, let's face it, in the old days producers were very much known to be burn artists. A lot of your most famous companies are still run by thugs and rip-off artists of the lowest order. But in the old days it was even worse. I've been shanked about five times over trying to collect money, and I was shot twice. I think just about anybody you talk to in this business—that shit has gone down on their head at some time or other, cause there just ain't no way of getting around that shit.

Junior Wells   It don't make no sense to go to the union with any complaints. The union ain't nothing but just somebody sitting on their ass to take your money. They don't get you no jobs or nothing. They say *one* thing: if someone don't pay you, he can't never have another union band in his place until he pays you. Well, hell! People don't give a damn if they have a union band or not. They can *always* get someone. The union ain't shit!

Louis Myers   I got a price and I don't go under that. But lots of cats will play for ten, eight dollars a night—throat-cutters!

The musicians' union done flopped out. Years ago, the union was a beautiful union—Local 208. They'd catch them throat-cutters and run them out. And I always had a gig: they used to call me up. But now they can't do this, because the majority of the musicians are these cats who can't play. And they's in the power.

So the union flopped. They can't protect me. All I got's a card. My card's all paid up, but . . . Tonight, you walk from bandstand to bandstand, you'll see. Ask those cats you find playing for their union cards. You'll find out: they ain't got no union cards.

Eddie Shaw—Mansfield, Conn., 1974

Eddie Shaw   You know, it's a funny thing: there's so many good musicians in Chicago, man, but there aren't enough of them on the road for the work that's there. Around Chicago there's no place to play. You got places for about ten bands to play in a big town like that. And there's forty or fifty bands in town. So lots of local fellows—good musicians who want to work—is out of work.

But they don't want to go out of town. They got families, really confined, and a lot of them say, "Hell, I need money; I'll get a day job." A-1 musicians. Wow! I know so many heavy cats in town, it's outasight!

But traveling bands have to pick up second, because they can't get the first choice. Lot of bands come around one time with one group and the next time around they got a whole new crew.

A club-owner can tell you. It's not that many traveling blues musicians to go around. You got fifteen to twenty good blues artists that got groups working on the road. Freddie King. Albert King. B. B. King. Muddy Waters. Howlin' Wolf. Junior Wells and Buddy Guy. James Cotton. Bo Diddley. John Lee Hooker. Hound Dog Taylor. Willie Dixon, who's just started out traveling again. Luther Allison that's doing *fair* now. Otis Rush. Jimmy Dawkins. Mighty Joe Young that teams up with Koko Taylor. Jimmy Reed, who's in and out. Johnny Littlejohn. Sonny Terry and Brownie McGhee. This girl from California—Big Mama Thornton got a pretty big band now. Charlie Musselwhite. Paul Butterfield and his blues band. Shakey Horton's getting him a band together and doing a few gigs now. Lowell Fulson is doing a few things. That's about all I can recall.

So from a club-owner's point of view, there's not enough good solid artists to fill fifty-two weeks—to bring in a winner every week. So clubs use the same artists three or four times a year.

So for the musicians who are willing to travel for work, it's better than fifteen years ago. Cause like now we're doing a lot of colleges and coffeehouses. A lot of hippie gigs on the road. But for the cats who won't leave Chicago—they can't find work.

Dave Myers   We been the Aces for more than twenty years and made a little name, but we've never done nothing great. Because, well, we've been more or less condemned-type guys, I guess. I don't know how to say that, but music hasn't really done me anything or done my brother Louis anything either, as fine a guitar player as he is. Because we never even moved. We haven't made no money. Really, I'm not gonna say I have. So all I've really got out of it is personal enjoyment—loving it and just doing it.

I've worked at the Keebler plant here in Chicago for ten years now cause I've had to. Music never contributed anything—no more than paying for my traveling and feeding me and clothing me on the road.

On records, they always want us to back other people up. Like the average agent will come to us now and ask the Aces to back their musician, but he ain't gonna use our name on the record. He's gonna say "So and So and Chicago Blues Band." And that's a condemned situation.

Sure, I'd like one day to make a little money playing, but shit! Boy, it's been rough. It's really been rough.

89

John Littlejohn—Chicago, 1974

John Littlejohn   I've been a mechanic off and on for
the last twenty years. I know a little something. I love
to hear the motors run. This is my life: it's between
music and grease.

Girls—I don't worry about them. Money I don't
worry about, because I know I ain't never going to have
none.

I likes to have fun and I just love my music. And I
sticks with it; I play it whether anyone listens or not.
Back in the fifties when I had my own shop, I used to
set in there by myself on Sunday with a bottle, and just
play my guitar and forget about everything that's out
there in the world . . .

George Smith—*Shaboo Inn,* Mansfield, Conn., 1973

George "Harmonica" Smith I usually get up about four-thirty; and sometimes I get up before then and go out on the street walking, because I'm *up-set.* I tear through the house, and I get out there walking, because I'm so wrapped up in this music thing. So I just walk with it, because I can't relax. Because I'm thinking about, what can I do? What can I do? What can I do to try and get my music out there like I seen others do? Why haven't I already been established? What is it? Is it something wrong with me?

But on the other hand, you are good enough to work with other artists as a sideman, but you're not good enough to get out and carry your own. What's wrong? What's wrong?

So you go over yourself and try to find out what the problem is. Is it something in *you?*

And that's a lot to think about.

James Cotton   B. B. King's about the onliest one in blues getting the recognition he's supposed to. And B. B. was out there twenty years before people found out he was B. B. King.

B. B. King

SWEET SIXTEEN

*When I first met you, baby, baby, you were jes' sweet
    sixteen.*
*Yes when I first met you, baby, baby, you were jes' sweet
    sixteen.*
*You'd jes' left your home then, woman, Lord, the
    sweetest thing I've ever seen.*

*But you wouldn't do nothin' baby, you wouldn't do any-
    thing I asked you to.*
*Yes you wouldn't do nothin' baby, you wouldn't do any-
    thing I asked you to.*
*You know you ran away from your home, baby, and
    now you wanna run away from ol' B. too.*

*You know I love you, I loved you before I could call your
    name.*
*Oh you know I loved you, baby, I loved you, I loved you
    before I could call your name.*
*Well it seems like everything I do now, baby, everything
    I do is in vain.*

*My brother is in Korea, baby, my sister is down in New
    Orleans.*
*Yes my brother is in Korea, baby, my sister is down in
    New Orleans.*
*Well you know I'm havin' so much trouble, woman,
    baby, I wonder what in the world is goin' to hap-
    pen to me.*

You know I love you, and I'll do anything you tell me to.
*Yes you know I love you, baby, baby, I love you and I'll
    do anything you tell me to.*
*Well there ain't nothin' in the world, woman, baby,
    there ain't nothin', nothin' in the world I wouldn't
    do for you.*

*You can treat me mean, baby, but I'll keep on wantin'
    you jes' the same.*
*Oh you can treat me mean, baby, well I'll keep lovin'
    you, I'll keep lovin' you jes' the same.*
*Oh but one of these days, baby, you gonna give a lot of
    money to hear someone call my name.*

B. B. King—New York City, 1973

John Lee Hooker I love women. Everybody do, if they's a man. But women'll make you drink; women'll make you do all *kind* of things! They're the reason a lot of guys get out and work. They work for women, give them their money; and the women mess over them and don't treat them right and start them to drinking. That's the key to this problem; *women* is the key. And that's for everybody; it ain't only for the blues singers. A woman can make *any*body sing the blues. She can turn your head around. I don't know why, but it's like that.

So that's my downfall and just about every blues singer's downfall. The average blues singer, he just can't keep a wife. He ain't *got* no wife, cause he's on the road all the time and his home gets tore up. You take like B. B. King: he had a lot of women problems—problem after problem. So anything he sings is about a woman.

If it wasn't for women, there wouldn't be no blues.

Willie Dixon In the beginning, Adam had the blues, cause he was lonesome. So God helped him and created a woman. Now everybody's got the blues.

[The following dialogue is excerpted from a joint interview with Sleepy John Estes and Hammie Nixon.]

Sleepy John Estes I'm married now to my second wife. I had three, but her husband come got the last one.

Hammie Nixon Everytime I'd get lucky and get me a wife, [Sleepy] John'd come along and say, "I got me a trailer and I want somebody to travel with me and play music." I'd say, "I just got married. I can't leave. I done messed up so much." I been married ten times. He done took me from all of them. And I'd do the same thing whenever he'd get him a good woman. We'd take off together and walk them dusty roads.

I married first time in twenty-nine. Only stayed with her about a month. Me and John running around so much, she said she didn't like no musician on the road for six months at a time. So me and her got separated.

In about three or four years, I married me another one. She was a pretty good girl. Me and her stayed together, in and out, for about nine years.

Then I married another one, a little old girl I got from Jackson, Mississippi. She did pretty good. All of them did pretty good. I just wouldn't stay home. Just run around too much to have a wife.

My fourth wife was a girl called Joanna. I started to make a crop with her; and John had him a wife then and he was gonna make a crop, too. So one day I looked up and seen him coming across the field with his old guitar swinging. When the sun get too hot, you know, he always step out. He said, "Hook your mule to the fence. Let's go." I done followed him out across the

Sleepy John Estes and Hammie Nixon—New York City, 1974

field, and we pulled off for Chicago, hoboing. So I put *her* down.

Number five stayed with me about six or eight months, I guess. I took off then for a year. She said I wasn't no good. She wanted to kill me. The last time I saw her, she was hitting at me with a razor.

Another one I stayed with two years, another six or eight months.

Mostly they worried me to death—they didn't want no musician staying on the road.

My second-to-last wife killed a man back a few months ago. She's a desperado. I married her around twelve years ago and we separated right away, but I just divorced her two years ago. Everyone back home told me to get rid of her, but I was all tied up with her and couldn't get away. She drank and cut up and went to the jailhouse so much. Every time I looked around, I had to pay a fine.

I got John's oldest daughter now. She's young and very quiet and she don't drink, and that's what I like. I got a bad boy by her. Worst little devil in the world. He's three, but he think he's old as I am. Sometimes he asks me, "Ain't I big as you?" He wants to drive my car even.

I got seventeen other kids, too, and about twelve grandkids: but I'll tell you the natural-born truth—I didn't have no kids by any of my *wives* but the last one.

Sleepy John Estes I got along best with one of Hammie's wives. She was so nice to me.

Hammie Nixon My second wife's name was Beatrice. I was running a milk dairy and going good. But this guy [Sleepy John Estes] always come around there. Him and Bea, they'd go fishing. I used to go milking and say, "Listen, John, you get out from here." He'd say, "When I get my breakfast, I'll go." He'd be still in bed. He helped her do the wash and all that stuff.

He took her away from me in the end, and, Lord, I hated him for a while. Wanted to cut him and see some of his blood.

Sleepy John Estes That child seemed like my sister to me.

Hammie Nixon Me and Sleepy John, we old sickly men now. We been beat out and run down and played music so hard. We been playing together over forty-five years, in the country, town, and everywhere. We know one another from A to Z.

We raise the devil at one another every little once in a while. Bucks against one another—I get mad at him, sometimes he cuss awhile and we threaten one another; but then he quiets down. Then *I* won't say nothing to him. Finally he'll call me, and I make like I don't hear him. And finally, I forget I was ever mad. He know how to handle me alright.

Sleepy John Estes I go and talk to him some kind of old scattertalk. He say, "Go away man, I ain't from no jungle." But I keep joking at him.

Esther Phillips I was never married. If you've been singing as long as I have, you'd think I would have tried it one time, right? But I've just never had the time—except for three relationships, and I'm working on the third one now.

When I was about eighteen, I really came close to marrying a guy. We eloped to Yuma, Arizona, and we got to the border and I said, "Unh uh." I just couldn't.

Now my guy—he's on me about this piece of paper that says we're married. That piece of paper means a lot to some people, but it don't mean nothing to me. Because I could marry you tomorrow and be the same—I may cuss you out at the wedding if you do something, you know. I cannot change. It's not that I have no respect for men. I love to cook, I love to make my man happy. But I work hard and I'm tired and I have to keep pushing. So just don't give me no shit.

When I'm with a man, I don't care about the way he looks. I care about where his head is at, how he thinks, what he wants out of life. And if he gets to talking off the wall, "Well, hey, if that's what you want, fine. But I'll see ya."

I have men, you know, who'll hit on me in clubs. But there's something about the way I carry myself, or the vibes I throw off when I'm working—they'll tell me how much they enjoy my singing, and I thank them, and if they're pleasant to talk to, I'll sit down and have a drink with them. And that's the end of that. I don't want a reputation of—see, men can do these kinds of things and get away with it. But that's something I never did anyway. I guess it comes from my religious upbringing.

When I was a little girl, I had a crush on our trumpet player. And after him I swore I would never ever even come close to marrying a musician. Until my last guy—the one I'm with now. He's a percussionist. But it's not such a bad scene, because he understands that I have something to do, and there's no heckling. I've tried dating guys who work nine to five, and they don't understand that when I have something to do, I have to do it. Then there's the natural problem of making more money in one night than he can in two weeks, and that really blows it. I've never found a way to solve that. And he might feel very much out of place being where I perform. Which means I have to devote most of my attention to him instead of doing what I should be doing. But with this particular musician that I'm with now, his only hangup, which he's kind of coming out of, is jealousy. Jealous or what, I'm here because I *want* to be here. And I think men should start to realize that about female entertainers—that they're there because they want to be.

I identify with parts of women's lib but I'm not throwing my brassiere away! I've been taking care of myself for so long, but I must have a man. Has to be a man in my life because everybody needs somebody. But I can identify with the housewife's attitude, the ones that sit at home all day, and they've got to have supper the minute he walks in, ready and hot. But most of all, I identify with the housewife who's qualified and wants a job, but he doesn't *want* her to have a job. And even if he doesn't mind, she cannot make the money a male can make, even if she's qualified. But as far as this male-chauvinistic pig stuff, I don't even have time to listen to that. Because I've been liberated all my life.

Eddie "Cleanhead" Vinson—New York City, 1973

Eddie "Cleanhead" Vinson

CLEANHEAD'S BLUES

Folks call me Mr. Cleanhead,
just because my head is bald.
Folks call me Mr. Cleanhead,
just because my head is bald.

But with the stuff that I use,
I don't need no hair at all.

If it wasn't for you women,
I'd have my curly locks today.
If it wasn't for you women,
I'd have my curly locks today.

But I been hugged, kissed and petted,
til all my hair was rubbed away.

When it starts to getting winter,
my head gets kinda cold.
I try to grow a little hair,
but I can't to save my soul.
When it comes to getting summer,
I get such a pretty tan.
You can hear all the women holler,
"Where can I find that Cleanhead man?"
Yes they call me Mr. Cleanhead,
cause I been bald a long long time.
But I don't need to worry.
You get yours;
And brother, you know I'll get mine.

James Cotton   I been married twenty years, man. My wife's a little bit different from me; she's a *home*-type woman. She like to stay and mind the kids. I've had my own band six years now, and she heard it play three times . . .

When we'd been together for a while, after I started traveling with Muddy Waters, I took her on a tour with us—ninety one-nighters. She stayed with it forty-five days, I think it was. She said, "Well, just send me home. I'll be there whenever you get there. Just always look for me at home."

Hound Dog Taylor I met my wife twenty-three years ago. She come to the club I was playing—her and a girlfriend. It was her birthday. She was sitting there, looking and looking, wearing a little white dress—she wasn't but a little bitty thing then, now she's about two hundred pounds, but she's okay—she's okay. So she kept looking at me. When we took a break I was standing over there watching her, wondering why she kept looking. I went over and started talking, said, "Hey, babe, how you doing?" and we talked. Then I took her home.

We sat in the car and necked for a while. That's all—just necked. I was pretty drunk, and it was the first time with her anyway. After she went in I sat there a long time. I could see two streets—had to get sober enough so's I could drive home. I'd've drove into the side of a house.

Next day she called me, and we been together ever since.

We get along fine—no problems. She don't bug me. I can be away three nights even when I'm in Chicago. I can come home at ten o'clock at night, she'll say, "You hungry? Want some coffee?" I take a job without much money, she don't bug me—just says, "Go ahead if you want to." Not like some musicians' wives. She just wants me to do what I like. Some cats are jealous of us . . .

Honeyboy Edwards I was married twenty-four years. I got my wife from Helena, Arkansas, and we moved all over Mississippi, Arkansas, Texas—she was with me everywhere I went. I losed her two years ago. I miss her, too.

My wife was young, really good-looking and everything. She wore good clothes, and she was so *friendly*.

Everybody that she see, she was laughing with them—just kept her mouth open, always talking, laughing; she had a smile on her face *all* the time. I had a sweet, lovely wife.

We didn't do nothing but just stay on the road. That's all we done. And get babies. Then she'd stay home during the week, but on weekends she'd get a babysitter and go with me.

Sometimes we'd work together. I started working in a club one night, and my wife was there, looking real good, all dressed up. And the clubowner said, "Is that your wife?"

I say, "Yes it is." So they offered her a job waiting tables and she started the same night. Put a little white cap and apron on. She was looking so nice, strutting around . . . We made some good money together, too.

But my wife had liver trouble. She had cirrhosis of the liver. That's like when whiskey *cook* your liver. See, she could drink and you'd never know she was drinking cause she never clowned or got loud. But when I'd go someplace to play, if she wasn't working too, she'd get a pint of whiskey, get a table, set out there and drink the whole thing by herself. When I got through, we'd go right home, lay down . . .

When she found out about the cirrhosis, it was too late. It turned into a heart condition, and then her heart got weak. And then she got short-winded—couldn't catch her breath. Foam would come up in her mouth. *Foam.*

Since I lose her, I don't run around too much. I'm getting old, and I can't stand too much bad living. We were young when we married, but we'd've been together right now—arguing and fussing at each other—if she'd've been living . . .

Bo Diddley I was married to a mean broad once. I woke up one night and that chick was sitting up in the bed looking at me, picking her fingernails with a brand new switchblade. Four thirty in the morning. I asked her what she was doing. She said, "I'm *looking* at you."

"Why you watching me sleep?"

"I'm just watching you, that's all." I had whupped her about two nights before that.

I divorced her. Damn right! She gonna sit up and watch me while I sleep? I ain't no baby. *I* knowed why she was watching me: she was trying to figure out where to start cutting.

Luther Tucker The reason I don't have a gun, or even a knife, now—it's too easy to use it. If you got a weapon, you have the tendency not to take as much as you would otherwise.

The last gun I had was when I was with my first wife. I had two chicks one night and they brought me home. I was kissing these chicks good night and my wife was standing in the doorway. So they burnt rubber leaving, and I went in the house. Then my wife and I had a big fight. After that I went to sleep—I'd been up all night. Well, my gun was at home—taken apart, bullets hidden. When I woke up, she'd found the gun, loaded it, and stuck it in my face. I was looking down the barrel. wow!

Hound Dog Taylor You'd be surprised: when you get older, you get a little more scared. But man, when I was young—boy, I was something! Whooo! I'd walk in a lion's den, it didn't make me no difference. But now I'm scared to go out the house less'n I got my pistol in my pocket. You *got* to carry a pistol in Chicago.

You can buy them new, you can buy them used. The trouble is, if you buy a used one, you don't know if it's clean or not. If you do something with it, throw it away and go get you another one. Someone else gonna pick it up and do the same thing. So it just goes round and round, round and round . . .

I don't bother no one. If I walked in a tavern and a cat was kissing my wife, I wouldn't say anything. I wouldn't say a word except, "Hey, baby, what's happening?"

I try to cool things off. A cat can call me anything he wants to, but if he lay a hand on me, he gonna get it. If he argue with me, I'll just look at him and walk away. Maybe even buy him a drink. But if he get ready to swing, he better get ready to die.

I'm fifty-eight years old, man. I can't let myself get stomped in the street.

Buddy Guy After you pass thirty-five, you begin to feel things that you used to didn't feel, especially living the night life of a musician. You can't get enough sleep unless you can sleep during the day, which I can't. I can stay out till 3:00 A.M., and still I can't sleep past daybreak, I guess cause I was raised on a farm. I leave Junior [Wells] sleeping and go have coffee in the van and read two or three newspapers until ten or so.

And when we're in Chicago between gigs, I watch that evening news at six o'clock, and I can't hardly even finish it; I am asleep before it's even over.

Buddy Guy and Junior Wells—Beverly, Mass., 1974

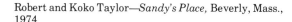
Robert and Koko Taylor—*Sandy's Place,* Beverly, Mass., 1974

Muddy Waters—*Crystal Lake Ballroom,* Ellington, Conn., 1974

Muddy Waters   I don't write much anymore—can't think. See, writing songs is something that has to come to you. Like when we talk, you and I, you can say a word, and I will put it in the back of my mind. I grab it, because you said a big word. We got talking one day, Pinetop, my piano player, and I, about some cat who was playing, and he said, "Ooh, man, that cat's *bopping* that thing!" Next day, I'm writing a song about bopping that thing. That's the way *that* goes.

I used to dream a song when I was really deep into it. But you got to get up from your dream and get it down, because otherwise, when you wake up in the morning, you ain't got it— it's *gone.* I'd dream and get up and wake my wife up and say, "Hey, baby, put this down *now!*" You know? I think I dreamed about the song "She Moves Me," and then I went and put some heck of a words into that thing.

But that was when I was younger. Age slows down your reflexes. I just can't think like that anymore. I used to say, "I'm gonna record." I'd get by myself about a day and get four songs ready for the studio. I didn't write down the tune, either. I'd be thinking, singing the song in my mind and playing my guitar right along with it.

That's why I tell people I'm getting old . . . I can't *think* it no more. You got to be young, young, young. And with a hell of a head on your body.

John Lee Hooker   I don't like to rhyme lyrics. I could; but if I rhymed it, I'd be just like all the rest of the blues singers. I *can* do straight twelve-bar blues, but it ain't me. I want to be different: I got a different beat from them; I rhyme different from them; *every-*thing's different.

But some songs I rhyme to the teeth. Like, "It Serves Me Right to Suffer"—I rhymed that one. "Boom, Boom"—I rhymed that one a little bit. But I usually let it all hang out. I just say it the way I feel it.

Word-by-word, lyric-by-lyric music—that's from the *book:* that ain't the way I feel. If I feel some way, I'm gonna let it come out. On my records, just like in the clubs, I make up the words right on the spot. It might rhyme and it might not. I don't care.

Eddie Shaw   What I like is to write lyrics. I'm mostly expressing a story instead of just saying, "Hey, baby, I love you. You sho' look good to me. I'm leaving this evening, won't be back till three." You know? I'm trying to tell more of a story from the beginning to the end. Like I may say, "Started in 1959 and I was broke and didn't have no shoes. And now it's 1974. Here I am with one million dollars." And I've told a story from the beginning right up to the end.

Koko Taylor   Singing is like a part of me. It's something I love to do—more than just a job. I can't think of anything I'd really enjoy doing more. So I spend most of my time trying to improve my singing.

But I'm spending more time trying to write lyrics, too. Willie Dixon says he's gonna help me with some tunes as soon as he gets a chance. The few songs I've written mean a lot to me, cause I discovered, "Hey, I can do it too!"

Brownie McGhee   I want to make people happy, because I want to be happy myself. People don't come to
see me cry. You can't stop somebody's heart from ach-
ing when *you* cry. So you got to fill them with joy. Or if
a song is sad, they want to see some beauty in that
sadness—not just teardrops.

Bob Riedy   There's one thing that makes the whole
thing worthwhile. One night a month, maybe two
nights a month, something clicks. You're playing and
you're not thinking and it's coming straight from your
feelings to your hands. That's what it's all about; you
get ad*dict*ed! That's how people get hooked on drugs.
They get that feeling, and they want it to happen
again.

Like the other night, we had one of those nights! I
was practicing the horn section I'm gonna use on the
next album. John Littlejohn was there; Hound Dog was
there; and suddenly everything was clicking. The lead
guitar was just right and John Littlejohn jumped in
and we did a rhythm thing and then I did a lead and it
just all built up and up and up.

From my level looking up to theirs, it seems like this
must happen for someone like Ray Charles or Aretha
Franklin every few nights. I know no one can feel it
every night. It can't happen; it's an impossibility. But
even if it only happens once a month, it's what makes
everything else you have to do worthwhile.

Brownie McGhee with fan—*Shaboo Inn,* Mansfield, Conn., 1974

Hound Dog Taylor   If you having a good time, everybody's gonna have a good time, too. Sho will! But if you mad up there, look like you sick, looking back there at him every time a man make a mistake—turning around—that's no good. You *nev*er supposed to turn your back on the audience.

I ain't never been fired since I been playing. Never have been fired, never had nobody take my job. I can go around any tavern in Chicago and take away the musicians' job. And they can come and play around me; I don't care. A lot of cats won't let other musicians on the bandstand with them, but I ain't like that.

I associate with everybody. People say, "Hey, Hound Dog!" I have fun with everybody; I get a crowd *every*where I go. I won't be playing a damn thing but people love it cause I act like I *feel* it.

That's the only thing I always say: "Let's have some *fun!*"

Buddy Guy   The first year I was traveling . . . was it sixty-seven? Right—the year my father passed. I played at the Ann Arbor Blues and Jazz Festival; and after playing maybe forty-five minutes, I started doing some tricks with my guitar, playing it with drumsticks and stuff like that. Someone from the audience hollered out, "You been watching Jimi Hendrix!" I didn't even know who he *was* back in sixty-seven, so I called back, "Who is that? And they thought it was a big joke.

So I went to find out who was this Hendrix. I went to Canada, and people said, "Wow! You're copying Jimi Hendrix."

Well, I just kept on trying to find out about Hendrix. Till I finally made it back to New York.

In New York, in steps Hendrix—with a tape re-

Hound Dog Taylor—*Shaboo Inn,* Mansfield, Conn., 1973

corder. He say, "I've been following you for years. I want to tape what you're doing."

I say, "Well, from what I been hearing, I've been following *you*."

He said, "Well, you and I know better. Don't pay no mind to those other people."

But I was being criticized. My manager was getting on me not to clown. "Why don't you just stand still and play the blues?" I *can't* stand still when I play a note that feels good to me.

I been playing blues and putting on a show with my guitar all my life. I learned these guitar tricks from Guitar Slim, T-Bone Walker, and all those cats in the South. This is what I saw when I was learning to play. Guitar Slim was a *mons*ter in this. It used to just gas me to see him do it. So I said, "If I ever learn, I'm gonna do that."

When I was mostly playing for Black audiences in places like Tennessee and Texas, they would sit there and wait for this, you know. But if I go out there tomorrow and clown on stage, somebody gonna call out, "You're doing Hendrix!"

But I really don't think I would've been recognized as much as I have been if I didn't clown, because everybody you meet can play. You got all these kids now are *play*-ing! I know some guitar players could wrap me up in one hand, and they come up and ask me if I can help them get work!

Look, *I* learned how to play this tune, *you* learned how to play it. And we're both sitting there playing it. Both sound good. So what can I do to get the edge on you? I keep the audience on the wonder. Maybe I take my guitar and go away for a while.

One time, I was playing in a club, and the crowd wasn't doing a damn thing but holding conversations. So I say to myself, "I got to *stop* this." I had a very long cord at that time. So I just started walking with my guitar—out through the crowd, out the door, and I caught a bus—still playing! And I had everyone in that club out there on the street!

Please believe me: you got to capture the audience some way!

Junior Wells—*Theresa's Lounge,* Chicago, 1974

Junior Wells   I don't understand how you can play good music and stand still. I just don't see that.

That was a problem I had the first time I went to Europe. I got booed in Germany, because I was moving around and playing. And they wanted to see me like Sleepy John Estes or Muddy, where you get a chair and set down and play. I can't play that way.

I told Horst Lippmann, the festival producer, "I'm ready to go home. They don't like my music."

He said, "Damn it, do it the way you want to do it!"

So I kept on doing it, and they finally got the message.

Me, I just can't be still when I'm playing. Artist and entertainer come together; it's all expressing myself.

Hound Dog Taylor   I know some cats, lotta rock cats, smoke that dope stuff, and man, they be out of it; they be in another world. I don't see no sense in it.

I drink whiskey. I been drinking whiskey ever since I can remember. When I was eight or nine years old— further back than that!—I was drinking whiskey. We used to make that whiskey with molasses and sugar. I used to steal it from my stepdaddy. Make me drunk.

You have to drink to stay in step. You get tired out— you get dried up. You ain't gotta get drunk; I *never* get drunk. When I get to feel good I let it stay up there till it die down, then I get it back up again. You can't make music if you ain't got no spirit.

Big Mama Thornton—New York City, 1974

Big Mama Thornton I don't use dope, I just stick with my Old Granddaddy 100 proof and my old moonshine corn liquor. Weeds, pills, needles—I don't need nothing like that jive to get out on the stage and sing. I drink, yeah. It makes me happy. But as for getting drunk, falling around on the streets—never!

When some jive bum comes up and asks me, "Would you like to be lit up?" I tell him, "Yeah. I got a match. You want to be on fire? I got a little gas around here. I'll burn you up."

I'm working at this one club. Here comes a cat. Comes up with a handful of weeds. Says, "Take your choice."

You know what I told him? " Best thing you can do is put those things in your pocket and get out of my face. Not only out of my face, but out of the place."

The owner come up and asked me why I insulted that man. I said, "If you think I insulted him, call him in your office and search his pockets." When I saw him next, he had this jive cat up in his hand, man, carrying him to the door.

I don't know why, they always think I . . . they always come to me . . .

Esther Phillips An addict's problem is one of trying to stay clean every day. And it's not easy. Because the urge comes and it goes. But I've found that this year, since things have really started to happen for me, the urge comes more and more often, and it's harder to fight—even after seven years.

If you talk to five reporters a day and that's all they want to talk about, that puts it on your mind. It's no secret that I was addicted. I mean, everybody knows it from here to London; I just don't want to talk about it. Then when you go to the clubs, there's somebody trying to put a bag in your hand. And that makes it harder for me to stay clean.

My mother always told me that some people are just like crabs in a tub, but she'd never tell me any further and I didn't understand. So one day we went crabbing and we took a great big tub, and we caught thirty-five or forty crabs. And I noticed that every time one would try to get out, another one would reach out and pull it right back down. And I said, "*That*'s what she's been telling me!"

Luther Allison—*Shaboo Inn,* Mansfield, Conn., 1974

Luther Allison   I was playing at this place called "The Back Door" in Ventura, California. I had a headache—real *big* headache. And I asked anybody in the audience, "Do you have an aspirin?"

Well, this girl say, "I got something that's not an aspirin but it's stronger, and it's better for you than aspirin." I didn't take the whole tablet because she says, "Don't take it all, just a touch."

I was *ac*id. And by me not knowing what's jumping off, all that shit hit me, man. I'm playing, and the goddamn guitar look like it's moving in my hand—the neck of the guitar was *mov*ing.

The people thought I was just having a hell of a time, but I was miserable, man. Maybe I was playing in the right place, but I think it's im*pos*sible for me to have been playing right. I didn't know what it was, but I knew I wasn't sick—.

And I thought, "What the hell I gone and done *now,*" you know. "If I ever get over this one, I will *never* get into it again." That stuff stayed with me six hours!

You know, I don't knock the people who get off on it as long as they ain't shooting up and shit. But not for Luther; I *had* my experience.

Brownie McGhee   I used to have to drink whiskey to get self-confidence to perform. People believed in me, but I didn't believe in myself.

And my playing was getting worse all the time, which I didn't realize it. I thought I was getting *better*.

Well, one day I spoiled half a recording session at Savoy Records. When I listened to the playback, I was ashamed of myself. I said after that, "No more whiskey in my studio. If anybody wants to drink *after* work, I'll buy."

I made that decision in the early 1950's. I realized I didn't have to get drunk to play my guitar, and I've had that faith ever since. I don't feel lost up on stage like I sometimes used to; and I get more sure of myself all the time.

Esther Phillips   When it really falls heavy on me is when I get home—when I'm finished work and I'm laying down and I can't sleep cause I have to unwind— I just have to unwind from all that excitement, whatever I've created. I usually don't get to sleep until about five or six in the morning.

It gets me down, I can't deny that; it does. I don't even know sometimes how I can make a show— I'm too tired to go across the *street*. But when I hit the stage, everything disappears. All of that just leaves me.

John Lee Hooker   I watch them. Then I feel their mood with them. I move with them. I get up and get to rocking with them, and after I get them going, I keep them going—higher and higher; I just don't let them down. I take them in complete command.

I get the real driving beat going. And when one or two of the crowd start moving, I start moving with them. And when they see me moving, *they* start to move. When I get into it, I feel good all over—higher and higher and higher; there's no limit.

I can look at them and tell whether I'm reaching them or I ain't reaching them; I can *read* them. And if I don't reach them on some songs, I reach back and get another. I can always knock them dead with "The Boogie," so I save it till last.

They call me the King of the Boogie.

J. B. Hutto   I ain't had girls faint yet when I play, but sometimes they holler pretty loud. . .

Esther Phillips—*Paul's Mall,* Boston, 1974

James Cotton   Listen! My father was a preacher. We used to go to church on a Sunday morning, and some preacher from another church would be invited over to my daddy's church. And those two guys'd just stand there and *preach*. You could feel it inside you. People got happy, man. I seen people up dancing in church and *shout*ing.

It's the same thing I see out here in blues clubs. People get happy. They *feel* it. It's a feeling from one human body reaches another one when it's right. The audience can feel what I'm doing, and they sure feel good to me.

When my mama gave me my first harmonica, I started playing the wrong things on it—blues which they didn't approve in church. If my mother had knowed what I would do with that harp, she never would've bought it for me. Never! This is the way older people believed. Like, I went home two or three years ago and this old lady that I been knowing ever since I was a kid told me I was gonna die and go to hell singing "reels," she called them. But there's a whole lot of things you can die and go to hell for besides singing the blues. I have respect for what these people believe, but *I* believe human beings are supposed to do what they want to do—what they *feel*. And I feel that this blues thing is what I was intended to do. My father was a preacher; I'm a blues singer.

I used to sing bass in the choir when I was little, and we *meant* what we was singing. Well, I still mean it with blues, and I give it everything I've got—like my father did, preaching. I'm doing like my daddy did, but I hold my services in clubs where you can get a drink.

Esther Phillips—*Paul's Mall,* Boston, 1974

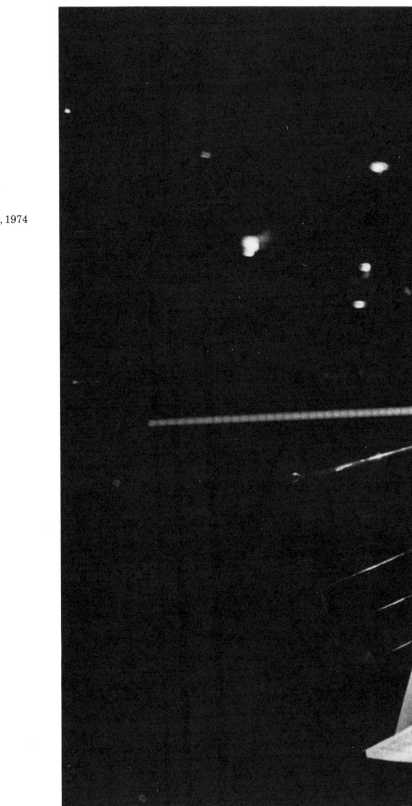

Kennard Johnson—Scotland, Conn., 1974

Kennard Johnson   Me and Charles Calmese will probably wind up getting a band together, and we're gonna stick to the blues. We're the start of a new generation of our type of Black blues.

You have the Allman Brothers, J. Geils, James Montgomery, and quite a few other White blues bands. Musically, our sound is the same—three chord changes—but there's a difference in it, a *big* difference, that's hard to pinpoint. I think our sound might be a little freer—free spirit music. I won't say which one is better; I respect these guys.

I've had people come up to me and say, "You looked me right in the eye while you were playing!" I know James [Cotton] does this all the time, and it sends a thrill through them. It's hard to explain: I guess we play our music to reach the inner soul of a person and make him feel happy.

John Lee Hooker There's a lot of good young White cats playing the blues and helping the blues along. There's Canned Heat: I made this big album, *Hooker 'n Heat,* with them. It's a boogying album. That was before this kid Al Wilson killed himself. He was a genius on harmonica. He was so wrapped up in it and wrapped up in *my thing.* He analyzed me—I dunno—like as a piece of gold or something. He just would work on my material all the time.

Then there's this J. Geils Blues Band. They do a lot of my stuff and they always credits me—"Written by John Lee Hooker." Magic Dick, Peter Wolf, J. Geils—I knew them when they was just getting started in Boston.

There's a lot of groups from England, too. I know all of them that's doing something because I used to stay touring over there six months out of the year.

John Mayall was my back-up band before he got famous. I was his idol. Also Eric Burdon's, too.

The Rolling Stones—they used to play second billing behind me before they got famous. We're still good friends. We partied and jammed together out in San Francisco when they come over here last time. We been trying to get together on an album. When I get over there next time, we'll work on it.

It may seem corny to you, but this is true: the groups from England really started the blues rolling and getting bigger among the kids—the White kids. At one time, fifteen years back, the blues was just among the Blacks—the older Black people. And this uprise started in England by the Beatles, Animals, Rolling Stones, it started *everybody* to digging the blues. It got real big over there, and then people in the States started to catch on. The last eight or ten years, I really been making it big.

121

Theresa's Lounge, Chicago, 1974

Lafayette Leake   I've gotten into big arguments with people that say these White cats can't play blues. I say they can—if they learn it. They used to say down South that a Black man couldn't operate this big heavy road equipment. The reason they said that was they didn't want to give him that job. It was just a tale. They used to say a Black man couldn't fly a jet plane. But the last time I went out to L.A., there was a Black guy flying my jet. And I can play Chopin, and he was sure White. I can re-create the sound he intended. Music is sound. When I listen to some guy from England singing the blues, I think sometimes he's colored. I can't tell the difference. Maybe it's not the original, but what's the difference in how it sounds?

You can write anything you can play, and people can play anything that can be written. There was a time they said blues and jazz couldn't be written, but that's untrue. I write blues all the time. And even the *feeling* can be written.

A lot of people don't understand this. Playing blues takes a certain amount of technique and coordination to get the right tone, but the techniques can be learned. There's no limit. They all own the same instruments. They all can learn to make bluesy *sounds*. The copy can be just as good as the original.

Blues, gospel, jazz—sure that was all created by Blacks. So maybe you'd rather see Blacks performing it, even if the imitators do just as well. I wish I could hear Chopin himself today, but I can't. So I have to listen to people playing what he wrote. But who knows—maybe they can play it better than he could.

Buddy Guy   We all got five fingers on each hand, and that's all it takes to play, man. The guitar don't give a damn about what color your fingers is.

Koko Taylor   My favorite audience is any one which digs blues. This is usually a White audience with a few Blacks. I've worked in strictly Black clubs for many years and always had to do a lot of soul, rock, and pop stuff to get over—you know, Aretha Franklin and Tina Turner. Let's face it, they don't want to hear the blues! Whereas White audiences will let me do my own thing all night long, which is blues. That's why I like doing concerts, festivals, college crowds and things.

I think it's a conforming thing with the Blacks. A lot of them deny the blues because they're ashamed of their past. They won't admit even if they really like blues—until they've had a few drinks.

Ann Arbor Blues and Jazz Festival in Exile,
Windsor, Ontario, 1974

Esther Phillips   I play with the audience. I *like* the
audience. They're full of bullshit, but they're a lot of
fun, too. They really are. If they get out of line, I just
stop singing. I don't cuss on stage; I just look at them.

You should be here tomorrow night [Saturday]. It's
gonna be a monster—the pimps and the whole funky
mob. Saturday night I draw a mixture of people you
wouldn't believe. I had a piano player to quit on me
because he said I drew the strangest people he had ever
been around. And then he quit—didn't want no money,
didn't give no notice. And I could understand it because I do; I just seem to draw a mixture of people,
man.

Since I got a new manager, she's not taking me
totally out of Black clubs, but she's trying to give me as
much White exposure as possible, you know, so I can
make some money. So she's been shooting me across
the line since May. I was getting *some* money in Black
clubs, but I wasn't like getting reviews and promotion
parties, you know—the way it should be done.

I never realized that the young White kids that are
coming up, man, they're altogether different from the
people in 1949, when they would keep the White kids
in the balcony and the whole floor was Black, and if the
White kids came out they would break the dances up.
And run us out of town. They did that in Biloxi, Mississippi. They did it in Baton Rouge, Louisiana. They
segregated the White kids from us, and I never realized
they would turn okay on me.

Black or White, they're all appreciative. The audience has always done something for me. Even in the
lean years, they still would come out to see me. I've had
followers all my life, and now it's their kids. I had a kid
come to the dressing room the other night, and he said,
"My mother knows you." He have me my whole history—the Johnny Otis days and everything.

The changeover is hard on me, though, because I was
never handled in this manner. You know, you wait for
something for twenty-five years and you think you are
totally prepared for it. Because you see other artists
getting this and getting that. But until *you* get it, you
don't actually know what they're going through. And
when you beg and you raise hell and you scream and
yell for something, and they say, "Okay, here it is,"
then you gotta deal with it. It's like an old saying at
Synanon they used to tell me: "Be careful what you ask
for because you just might get it."

Bo Diddley   As a rule, Black people don't follow me. *Period.* My folks are strictly anti-Bo Diddley. A few of them will come around cause they're curious to see is he doing the same old chinkety-chink-chink. They can't understand why I'm still here nineteen years later.

At first, I had a lot of Black fans; but after "Hey, Bo Diddley" they all disappeared. They held on for about three or four records. After that, I guess I got monotonous. I could tell that I was losing the crowds when they started dropping off to two or three hundred. Sure enough . . . So I said, "There's nothing for me to do but shoot for the other side of the fence."

I'm really hurt by it, man. It hurts me that I can't even draw my own folks and I'm playing *our* music. I'm accepted as a brother but they just don't go out to see Bo Diddley.

Blues and the stuff I was playing was supposed to be putting our people back fifty years. I used to hear all this crap. Muddy Waters and all of us was supposed to have been a disgrace to the race for playing blues.

It used to be a no-no to call me "Black." Now if you *don't* call me Black, you're liable to get killed. So I'm really in a crossfire. I'm really confused. I am totally confused.

Sunnyland Slim   I didn't know nothing else *but* the blues, and church songs, when I was coming up. They were singing the blues in Louisiana, Mississippi, Georgia, Florida, ever since there was a world, to my knowing. They sang on the prisoner camps and levee camps. People on the county farms cutting trees with an ax sang, "Ooh, Captain." It just sound good. People stand out for miles along the railroads and highways—chain gangs—singing, "Ooh, it ain't gonna rain no more, yeah." This was the blues . . . it had a sound to it.

What else could I come up knowing but the blues?

Sunnyland Slim—Chicago, 1973

Son Seals—Chicago, 1974

Son Seals At this point in my life, I don't think anymore along the lines of trying to learn from other guitarists. I enjoy listening to a lot of musicians, but I'm not into this thing where I run home, grab my guitar, and try to do what I just heard. I want to create my *own* stuff, my *own* version of the blues.

Through the years my mind has been growing. I feel like it's just like a piece of earth. It ought to be fertilized and strong enough by now and with enough material to create my own stuff. Just like raising a new crop every year. All I have to do is just cultivate it enough to make it bear.

I've listened to myself and I've said, "That's on the right track to where I want to be going." But I find myself still searching for *something*. I'm satisfied with what I do when I do it, you know? There's no doubt in my mind—it feels good and sounds okay. And the audience responds. But now still, I have a halfway mixed-up feeling about it.

I believe that the sound I'm trying to create has got to be different from anything I've played yet, in order for me to be completely satisfied. Maybe I'll *nev*er be satisfied, but I'll keep on trying to do something different. And I believe it's gonna happen—or I'm gonna bust my brains open, trying to think.

If you notice, when B. B. came out with his version of the blues, there wasn't none other like it. And up until today, there are thousands of musicians still playing along that same pattern of blues. B. B.'s style is great. But at the same time, if I was to continue the rest of my life trying to imitate him, well, I might as well do what lots of others have done—call myself B. B. King, Junior, too.

Now what I'm thinking is—if they try to sound like

B. B. King, well, why not one day they sound like Son Seals? I be thinking—can I some day be responsible for the blues changing?

So this is what I want to get across—me, *Son;* not Son and B. B. wrapped up into one. Just Son. This is what I want to do.

Hound Dog Taylor   When I die, people's gonna say, "He couldn't play shit but he sure made it sound good!"

Freddie King I want to get into producing things, like old blues musicians that people have forgotten. People who helped me. I produced one on Jimmy Rogers, the last one he did: "Go Tell Bird." I produced that, and it was a really good album. I played some guitar on two or three of the tracks—.

And then I'd like to do a mixed album of old musicians like Eddie Taylor, Robert Junior Lockwood, Hound Dog—people like that. I'd like to produce it myself. Here's the reason: I been listening to these guys play all my life, and I know what they want. I know *exactly* how they want to sound.

Now, the average recording company, when they get ready to record a cat like Wolf or John Lee Hooker, they will get some kid about nineteen or twenty years old to produce it. He don't know what the hell he's doing; he just started playing yesterday. He don't know what the guy *wants*. Like this Canned Heat produced this thing on John Lee. Good album! Really, I dug it. But it just don't sound like John Lee. Only thing you need with John Lee is give him his guitar, give him a piano player, and a drum, and a bass. And mostly just let him have it himself. Not too much psychedelic stuff. Wolf's record, the one he done in London—Clapton done this. Now, that was very good, too, and Clapton, he's a good musician. He's not no kid. He knows what he's doing. But what I mean is—well, take when Johnny Winter first started recording, they got Willie Dixon to do some blues, some real lowdown *blues,* go get Willie.

I'm just saying . . . alright, I've been in the field about seventeen or eighteen years. Alright, now, there's a kid just started playing last year. He had one, maybe, million seller. They want him to produce a thing on me. He don't know what I want. I could do it better myself;

I wouldn't *let* him produce it. Look here: Muddy been in the business longer than me; B. B. King been in the business longer than me. So if B. B. say to me, "Man, look, I'd like to produce a thing on you. I got some songs are *good,*" I'm ready! He *knows* what I want. But, now, here comes a cat, don't have no background, lucky enough to get a couple records—No, man.

Bob Riedy For our band's lead artists, we bring in veteran bluesmen. A lot of these guys are like diamonds in the rough, and we try to bring out their very best points. I feel that no matter what, any bluesman should be able to come into the club, any night, and we should be able to back him up—play his repertoire as good as anybody can.

For us, it's a musical apprenticeship. See, we're trying to expand our musical language. It's like writing: the more words and phrases you have to work with, the better you can express yourself. And the more notes, the more licks you have, the closer you get to hitting it on the head.

If I learn the total blues language and play it for years, eventually I hope I'll get to the place where I won't be thinking about it—I'll be doing it naturally. I want to talk with that accent for the rest of my life. If I end up playing jazz when I'm sixty, I still want that blues accent to be there.

So I'm gonna play this music no matter what. These bluesmen aren't gonna be around forever, so the time I spend on this now is an investment in the future. People say to us, "Why don't you play Paul Butterfield," or, "Why don't you play more stuff by Bloomfield?" Well, why should we? Why should we learn it secondhand when the men *they* learned from are still around?

Freddie King When I first went to Atlantic, King Curtiss was the producer, and he'd just let me do exactly what I wanted. I *knew* what I was after. See, I had done a lot of studio work as session man, like with Howlin' Wolf. Like on "Spoonful" and "Howlin' for my Darlin'," that's me on guitar. And when I first recorded for King, I had about six hits in a row. Songs like "Hideaway," "I Loved a Woman," "Got to Love with a Feelin'," "San Jose," "Jest Pickin'," "T. C. Baby," "Have You Ever Loved a Woman?" There was nobody around telling me what to do, and these was all hits.

But then they got smart and told me what to do and what to sing. And then I just fell off.

I been playing blues all my life. Some cat comes along. Wants me to play pop. Play some "Stardust." He tells me, "You know, it's hard to sell blues." I say, "Man, you got to be crazy. It's just the way you push. If you push blues, it'll sell." Because Eric Clapton done got rich off it twice or three times. Johnny Winter got rich. Fleetwood Mac, Peter Green, John Mayall. That's all they play is blues. And he tells me the blues don't sell. That's crazy—a bunch of bull.

But if a guy walks up with a song and says, "How'd you like this song?" Like Leon Russell, he writes some good stuff; and we work *together* in the studio. You listen to those last three albums I got out, how good they sound. That's *Gettin' Ready, Texas Cannonball,* and *Woman 'Cross the River.* This is where we go into the studio, sit down, and work together. Not somebody saying, "No, do this, do that, sing this song here." Then you can't feel it right. So really, I just don't do that anymore. If I don't like a song, I won't mess with it.

Doctor John—*Music Hall,* Boston, 1974

Doctor John I have hope to see the future of blues head more in the direction of more down home stuff. It's just lately that people are starting to really dig into some of the artists who are really talented but that has never had the opportunity to record—like some of these people in penitentiaries.

I've always believed that really the top groups is not the ones that get to record but them little groups that play in those little juke joints. It's just honest, innocent music, man. It's really playing the blues, with no name or recognition or nothing. These are the cats that are the authentic down home gut bucket.

I like what Taj Mahal did. He didn't grow up in the old blues school, but he went back there to dig.

A lot of these kids is doing that and bringing something back into the blues that was lost somewhere for a long time. When I first came up, the blues I was playing was almost be-bop orientated—very hip shit. Now it's going back beyond that to some kind of roots, which is a good thing.

The only problem is, once this innocent music gets known, the commercial people start making it slick and uptown. It's hard to avoid. I'm gonna tell you, it happened on me so fast, I didn't even realize it. It's a thing you get caught up in. All of a sudden people are telling you, "Hey man, look, try this, do this. . . ." And all of a sudden you're doing things just to be commerciable, which is really a fucked way of doing things. But that's business, cause the people that run the music business are just like people peddling soap or anything else. They don't give a shit about the product, as long as it'll sell.

When I heard that B. B. King record "Ghetto Woman" with all them damn violins . . . It might've been a hit and got B. B.'s name notorized, but to me that ain't B. B. and it ain't blues. I'm not knocking the artist. I'm just knocking this business that does that shit with records.

The shit that really ranks though is the mixing-up with the wah-wah pedals, and tremulo, and phase shifters and all these electronic gadgets. Going in and overdubbing and all that jive doesn't necessarily add up to something being good and qualified. I'd rather hear something that's true and spontaneous. I even like to hear mistakes, cause they make it like all the more real. That other electronic takeover turns me off drastically.

Louis Myers—*South Park Lounge,* Chicago, 1974

Little Beau Sharif   What's keeping the blues alive now is that Whites have started listening to it and are supporting it. Blues musicians are working hard to give blues to these people, and it's got to progress. Don't nothing stay the same.

The Whites are gonna contribute to the blues; they are *already*. They're understanding the blues. The music is just chords going round in a circle. They're learning that, and they're learning about the life of the Black.

And the Negro likes the blues; you can tell that from the audience. But he don't go *out* for it cause he'd *had* it, you understand what I mean?

But I figure maybe something'll come up out of it that'll catch *both* the races. See, you don't have so much segregation anymore, and a lot of the Blacks is feeling a little bit more comfortable. The Negroes always have wanted to get along with the White, but it's the Whites that's coming around now. And all this is involved in your musical thing. There's mingling of Black and White now. Both are gonna contribute, exchange ideas. And it's good. It's good. It's *good*.

Louis Myers   Younger kids hear more than other people. They don't miss no things. And they never forget what they hear. And this is what keeps music going on and on and on.

When the young be left out, there ain't nothing. In the last ten of fifteen years in the blues—nothing!

The blues has no future. You got people out here that's supposed to be representing the blues that never *was* representing no blues. They got a hell of a name, and it's a shame. So the blues has got to die. They're promoting it for the money but they know who to drop when times get tough. And that's what'll happen to the blues. When it stops making money, the promoters will cut it all loose. It'll just die overnight.

Willie Dixon   I got fourteen kids. All of them play music, even the three-year-old. All of them play blues.

Louis Myers I don't want my kids to waste their time playing blues. You can't make the money in blues. If they want to go to school and study music—that's different. If you can read and arrange and write music and you got a degree from music—then you got it made.

But blues is not like that. Only people making anything in blues is people who is out for some money and have some money behind them. I know hundreds of cats who try to play blues around here who got no backing. They ain't even working—can't even get round coin.

I love to play blues, man; but if I can't make no money, I got to do something else—I got to have a day job. I play blues because I love it, but it's all over so far as I'm concerned. I still can play; but it ain't nothing I can put my hand on and say, "This is it!" And I won't point my kids to it.

Pinetop Perkins I'll tell you about the blues. The blues ain't going out. The blues go down, come right back up again. The blues don't go *out*. There's *al*ways gonna be blues.

Luther Tucker   My son is two years and three months, and I'm very happy with him. He practice the guitar more than *I* do!

He says, "Guitar."

I say, "Okay, Baby, go get it."

He opens it up and starts playing on it—plays on it for hours. I'd sure like to get him one. He don't want no small guitar, though; he wants a *big* one.

He walks around the house singing. It's amazing coming from a child two years and three months old! I think he's gonna be a musician. I'd love to see that.

By the way, I also have a son Luther Danny Tucker; he's nineteen years old now, and he blows a flugelhorn. He won a music scholarship to college—plays drums, piano, sax, clarinet—everything but what I could help him with. He never did pick up the guitar.

He blows jazz, and he's trying to get me to play it, too. I say, "No, you got to play some blues. I been playing these blues too long to change now."

J. B. Hutto   Blues was the *original* thing! It come from church songs and they sung it from there. Then people wrote the soul part out, put in a rhythm, and that's where the blues comes from. They was trying to kick blues down and bring up this here rock and roll—I call it humping music—but they can do what they want: the blues will never die cause it's the original thing. It's coming back up from where they tried to stomp it down; it's coming back up again, and it's gonna get better. Blues will be blues until the world ends!

J. B. Hutto—Harvey, Ill., 1973

NOTES

Luther Allison
Born: Mayflower, Arkansas 1940
Lives: Miami, Florida
Instrument: Guitar, vocals, harmonica

Carey Bell
Born: Macon, Mississippi 1936
Lives: Chicago, Illinois
Instrument: Harmonica, vocals

Fred Below
Born: Chicago, Illinois 1928
Lives: Chicago, Illinois
Instrument: Drums

Buster Benton
Born: Texarkana, Arkansas 1933
Lives: Chicago, Illinois
Instrument: Guitar, vocals

Elvin Bishop
Born: Glendale, California 1942
Lives: San Francisco, California
Instrument: Guitar, vocals

Lonnie "Guitar Junior" Brooks
Born: Division, Louisiana 1933
Lives: Chicago, Illinois
Instrument: Guitar, vocals, throat harmonica

Clarence "Gatemouth" Brown
Born: Orange, Texas 1924
Lives: Aztec, New Mexico
Instrument: Guitar, vocals, violin, mandolin

George "Mojo" Buford
Born: Hernando, Mississippi 1927
Lives: Minneapolis, Minnesota
Instrument: Harmonica, vocals

James Cotton
Born: Tunica, Mississippi 1935
Lives: Chicago, Illinois
Instrument: Harmonica, vocals

Jimmy Dawkins
Born: Tchula, Mississippi 1936
Lives: Chicago, Illinois
Instrument: Guitar, vocals

Bo Diddley
Born: McComb, Mississippi 1928
Lives: Los Lunas, New Mexico
Instrument: Vocals, guitar

Willie Dixon
Born: Vicksburg, Mississippi 1915
Lives: Chicago, Illinois
Instrument: Vocals, bass

Doctor John
Born: New Orleans, Louisiana 1941
Lives: Los Angeles, California
Instrument: Vocals, piano, guitar

Honeyboy Edwards
Born: Shaw, Mississippi 1915
Lives: Chicago, Illinois
Instrument: Guitar, vocals

Sleepy John Estes
Born: Ripley, Tennessee 1903
Lives: Brownsville, Tennessee
Instrument: Vocals, guitar

Buddy Guy
Born: Lettsworth, Louisiana 1936
Lives: Chicago, Illinois
Instrument: Guitar, vocals

Phil Guy
Born: Lettsworth, Louisiana 1942
Lives: Chicago, Illinois
Instrument: Guitar, vocals

Ted Harvey
Born: Chicago, Illinois 1931
Lives: Chicago, Illinois
Instrument: Drums

John Lee Hooker
Born: Clarksdale, Mississippi 1917
Lives: Oakland, California
Instrument: Guitar, vocals

Lightnin' Hopkins
Born: Centerville, Texas 1912
Lives: Houston, Texas
Instrument: Guitar, vocals

J. B. Hutto
Born: Augusta, Georgia 1926
Lives: Harvey, Illinois
Instrument: Guitar, vocals

Kennard Johnson
Born: St. Louis, Missouri 1951
Lives: Chicago, Illinois
Instrument: Drums

Luther "Snake Boy" Johnson
Born: Davisboro, Georgia 1934
Lives: Dorchester, Massachusetts
Instrument: Guitar, vocals

B. B. King
Born: Itta Bena, Mississippi 1924
Lives: New York, New York
Instrument: Guitar, vocals

Freddie King
Born: Gilmer, Texas 1934
Lives: Dallas, Texas
Instrument: Guitar, vocals

Sammy Lawhorn
Born: Little Rock, Arkansas 1935
Lives: Chicago, Illinois
Instrument: Guitar

Lafayette Leake
Born: Wynomie, Mississippi c. 1920
Lives: Chicago, Illinois
Instrument: Piano, organ, vocals

John Littlejohn
Born: Lenox, Mississippi 1931
Lives: Chicago, Illinois
Instrument: Guitar, vocals

Robert Junior Lockwood
Born: Marvell, Arkansas 1915
Lives: Cleveland, Ohio
Instrument: Guitar, vocals

Brownie McGhee
Born: Knoxville, Tennessee 1915
Lives: Oakland, California
Instrument: Guitar, vocals

Little Brother Montgomery
Born: Kentwood, Louisiana 1906
Lives: Chicago, Illinois
Instrument: Piano, vocals

Matt "Guitar" Murphy
Born: Sunflower, Mississippi 1929
Lives: Chicago, Illinois
Instrument: Guitar

Dave Myers
Born: Byhalia, Mississippi 1926
Lives: Chicago, Illinois
Instrument: Bass, vocals

Louis Myers
Born: Byhalia, Mississippi 1929
Lives: Chicago, Illinois
Instrument: Guitar, harmonica, vocals

Hammie Nixon
Born: Brownsville, Tennessee 1909
Lives: Brownsville, Tennessee
Instrument: Harmonica, jug, tub bass, washboard, vocals, kazoo

Pinetop Perkins
Born: Belzoni, Mississippi 1913
Lives: Chicago, Illinois
Instrument: Piano, vocals

Esther Phillips
Born: Galveston, Texas 1935
Lives: Los Angeles, California
Instrument: Vocals, piano

Bob Riedy
Born: Casco, Wisconsin 1946
Lives: Chicago, Illinois
Instrument: Piano, organ

Son Seals
Born: Osceola, Arkansas 1942
Lives: Chicago, Illinois
Instrument: Guitar, vocals, drums

Little Beau Sharif
Born: Atlanta, Georgia 1924
Lives: Chicago, Illinois
Instrument: Tenor sax

Eddie Shaw
Born: Greenville, Mississippi 1936
Lives: Chicago, Illinois
Instrument: Tenor sax, vocals

Johnny Shines
Born: Frazier, Tennessee 1915
Lives: Holt, Alabama
Instrument: Vocals, guitar

Sunnyland Slim
Born: Vance, Mississippi 1907
Lives: Chicago, Illinois
Instrument: Piano, vocals

George "Harmonica" Smith
Born: Cairo, Illinois 1924
Lives: Los Angeles, California
Instrument: Harmonica, vocals

Little Willie Smith
Born: Helena, Arkansas 1936
Lives: Chicago, Illinois
Instrument: Drums

Roosevelt Sykes
Born: Helena, Arkansas 1906
Lives: New Orleans, Louisiana
Instrument: Piano, vocals

Hound Dog Taylor
Born: Natchez, Mississippi 1915
Lives: Chicago, Illinois
Instrument: Guitar, vocals

Koko Taylor
Born: Memphis, Tennessee 1938
Lives: Chicago, Illinois
Instrument: Vocals

Sonny Terry
Born: Greensboro, Georgia 1911
Lives: Holliswood, Long Island, New York
Instrument: Harmonica, vocals

Big Mama Thornton
Born: Montgomery, Alabama 1925
Lives: Los Angeles, California
Instrument: Vocals, harmonica, drums

Luther Tucker
Born: Memphis, Tennessee 1936
Lives: San Anselmo, California
Instrument: Guitar, vocals

Eddie "Cleanhead" Vinson
Born: Houston, Texas 1917
Lives: Houston, Texas
Instrument: Alto sax, vocals

Muddy Waters
Born: Rolling Fork, Mississippi 1915
Lives: Chicago, Illinois
Instrument: Vocals, guitar

Junior Wells
Born: Memphis, Tennessee 1934
Lives: Chicago, Illinois
Instrument: Vocals, harmonica

Joe Young
Born: Shreveport, Louisiana 1927
Lives: Chicago, Illinois
Instrument: Guitar, vocals

INDEX